## Introduction

Within the pages of this book you will find 50 original and vintage stained glass windows designs, taken from various Churches and Cathedrals around the world to colour in using your own creativity and imagination.

Many of the designs feature religious and historical characters and have been reproduced here in black and white for your colouring enjoyment.

NOTE: I have attempted to replicate these images as close to the originals as possible and, as such you will find that many of the images have shaded areas, as well as thick black outlines around them. However, these can be lightly coloured over with pencil or another method of your choice if desired.

Finally, I decided to create this book because I have had a keen interest in original and historic stained glass windows for a few years now. I hope that you will find this book both enjoyable and fun to colour in.

Why not share your finished designs with others?

You can also find more FREE patterns and designs on my Facebook page below as well as share your completed pages with others too.

**https://www.facebook.com/Best-Adult-Coloring-Books-1497039227284351**

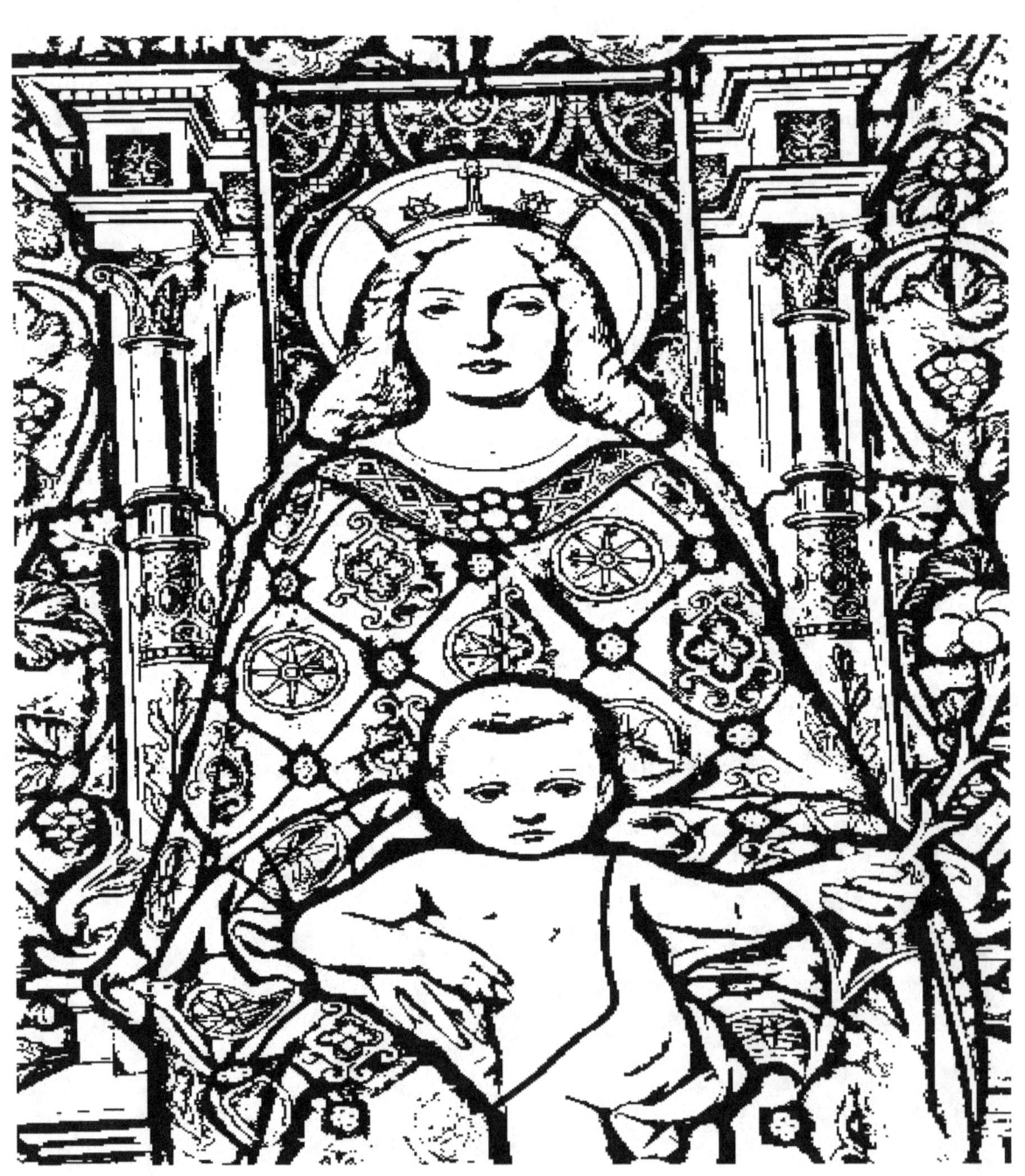

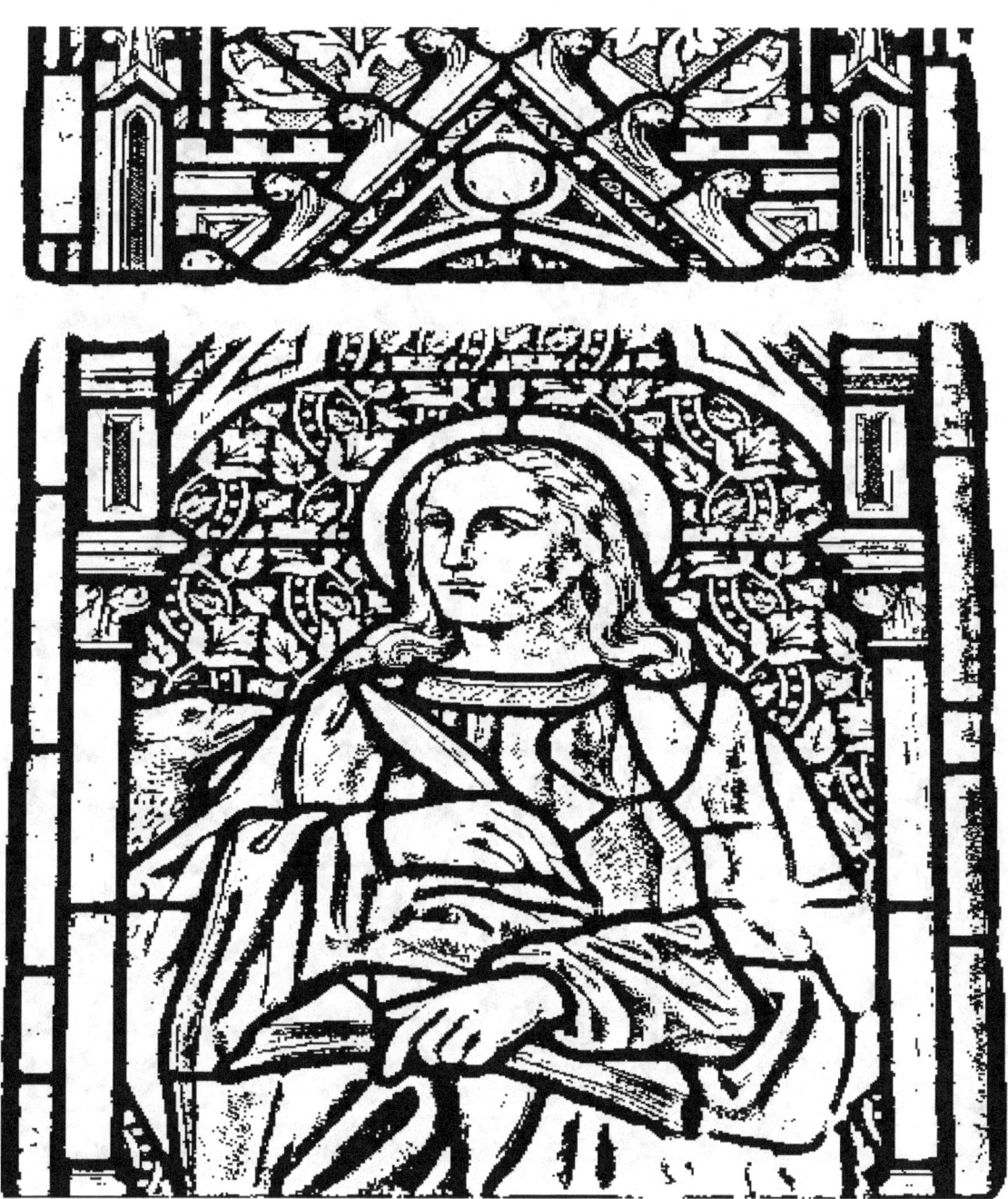

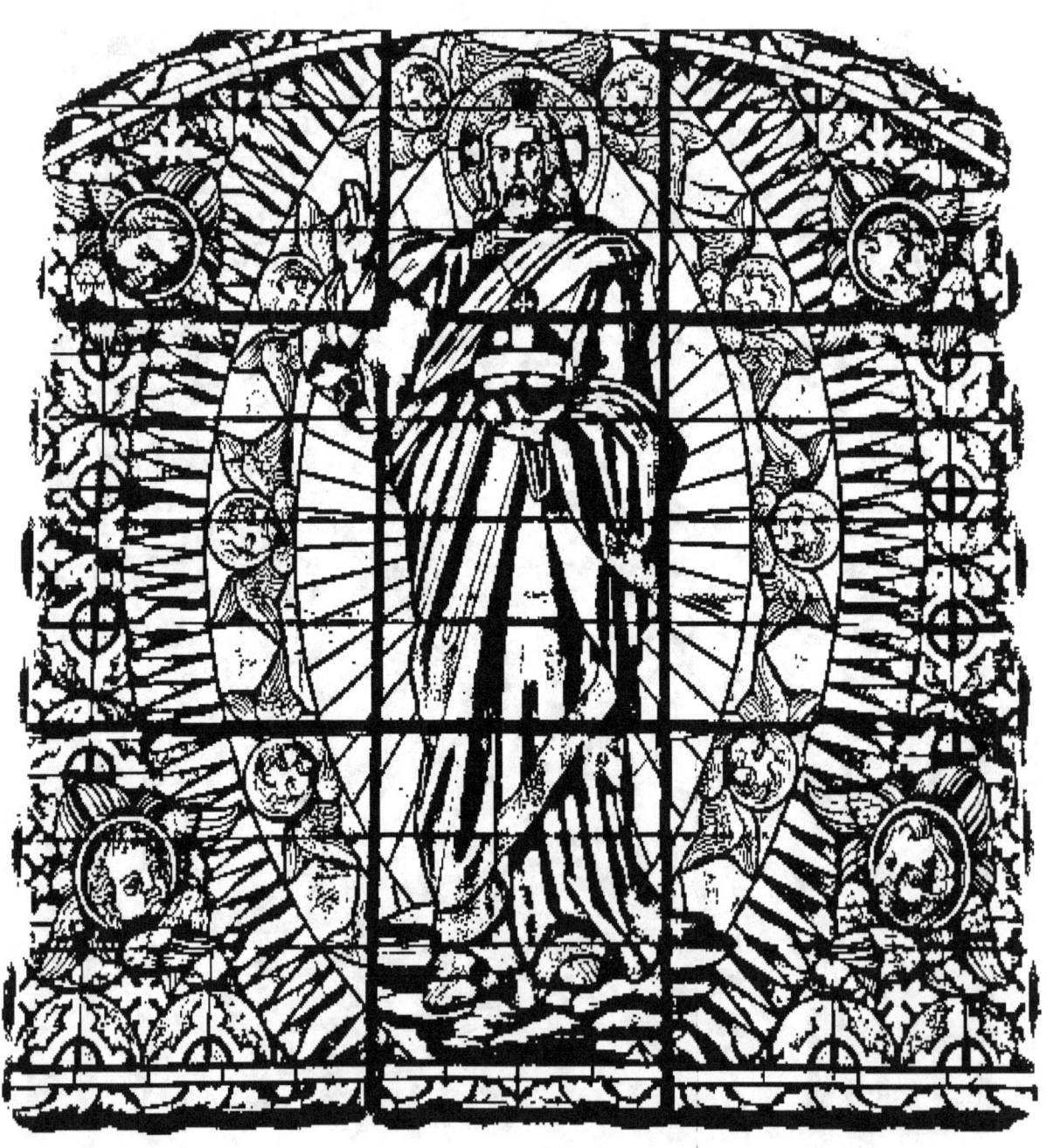

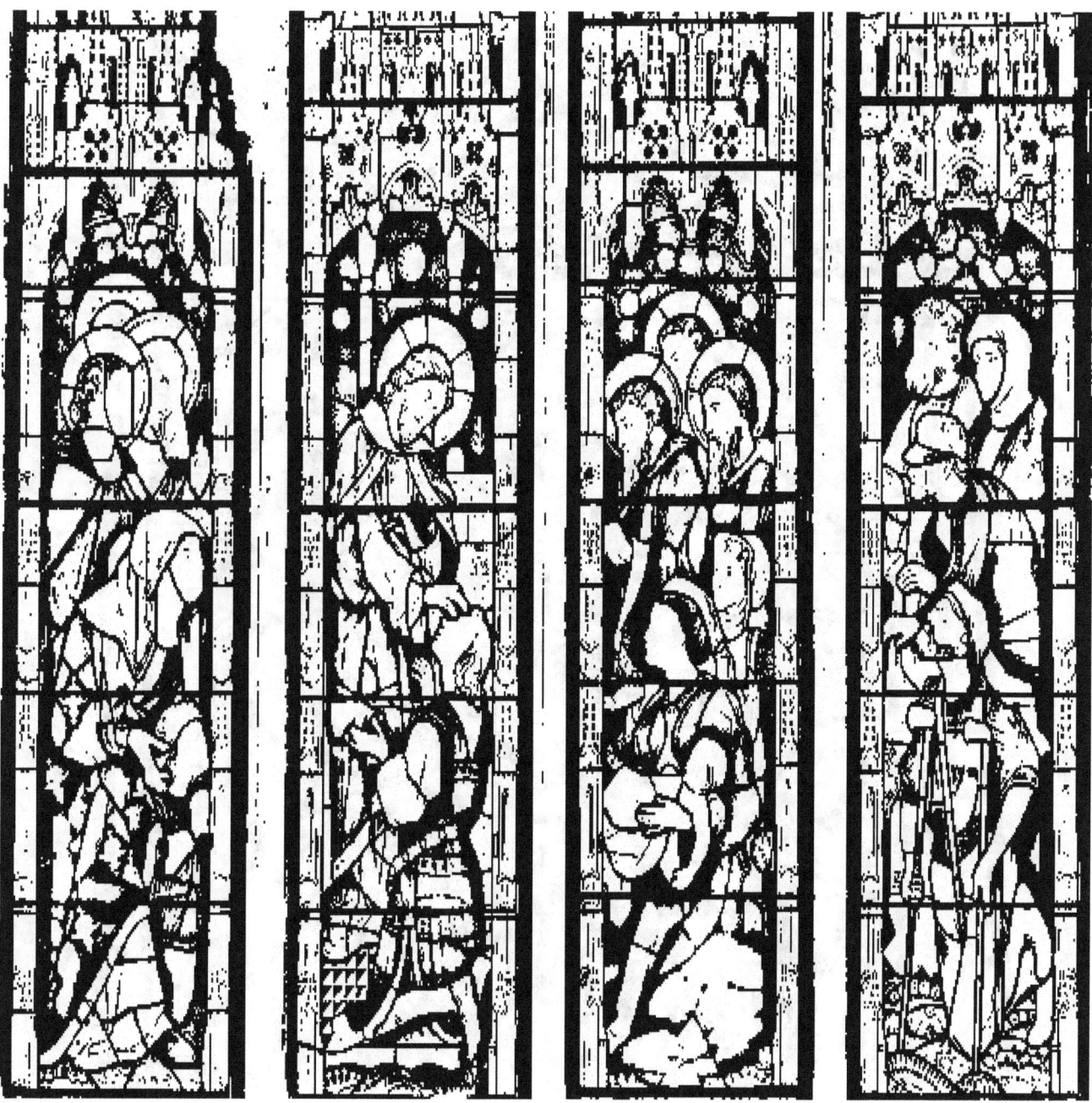

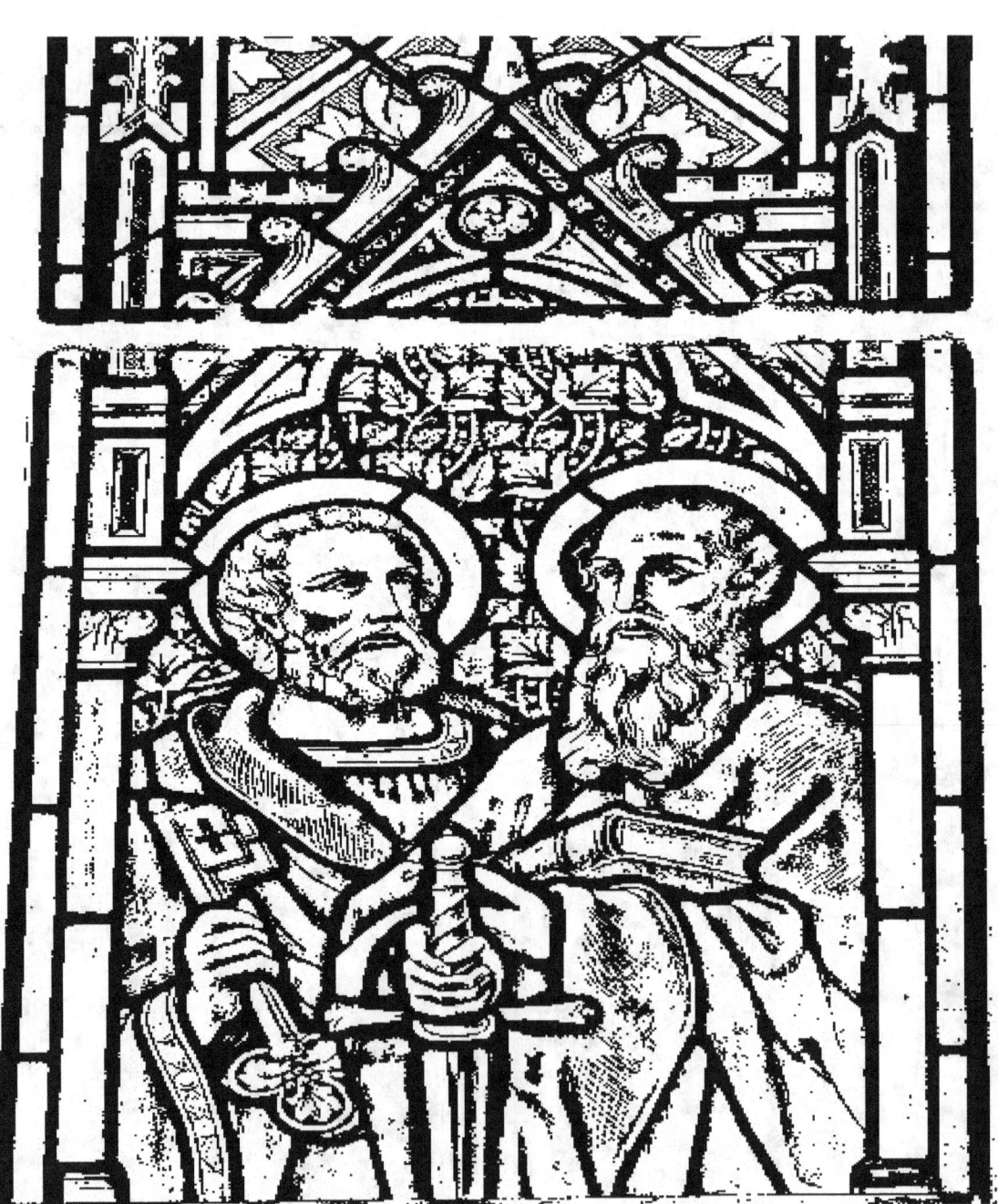

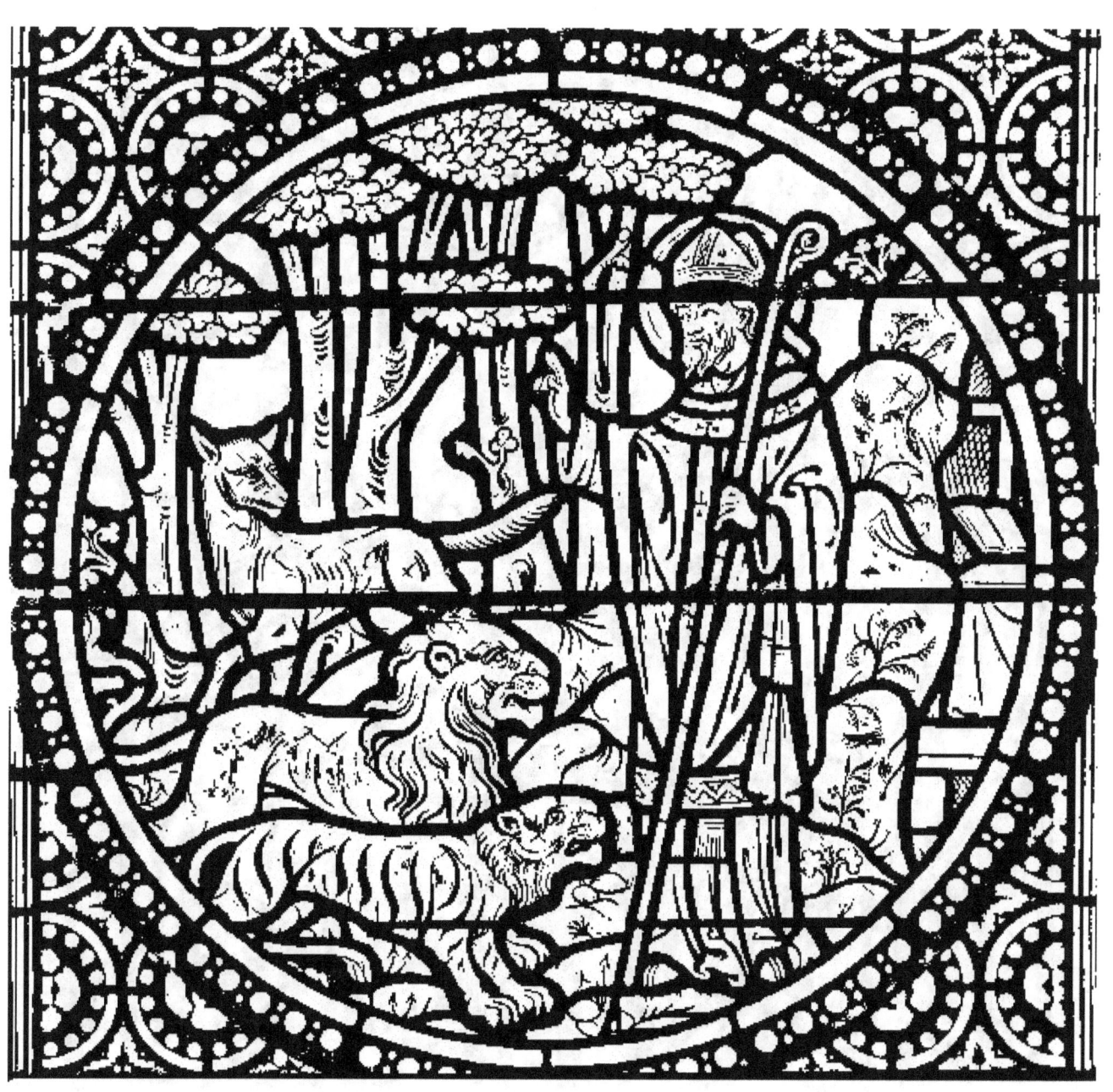

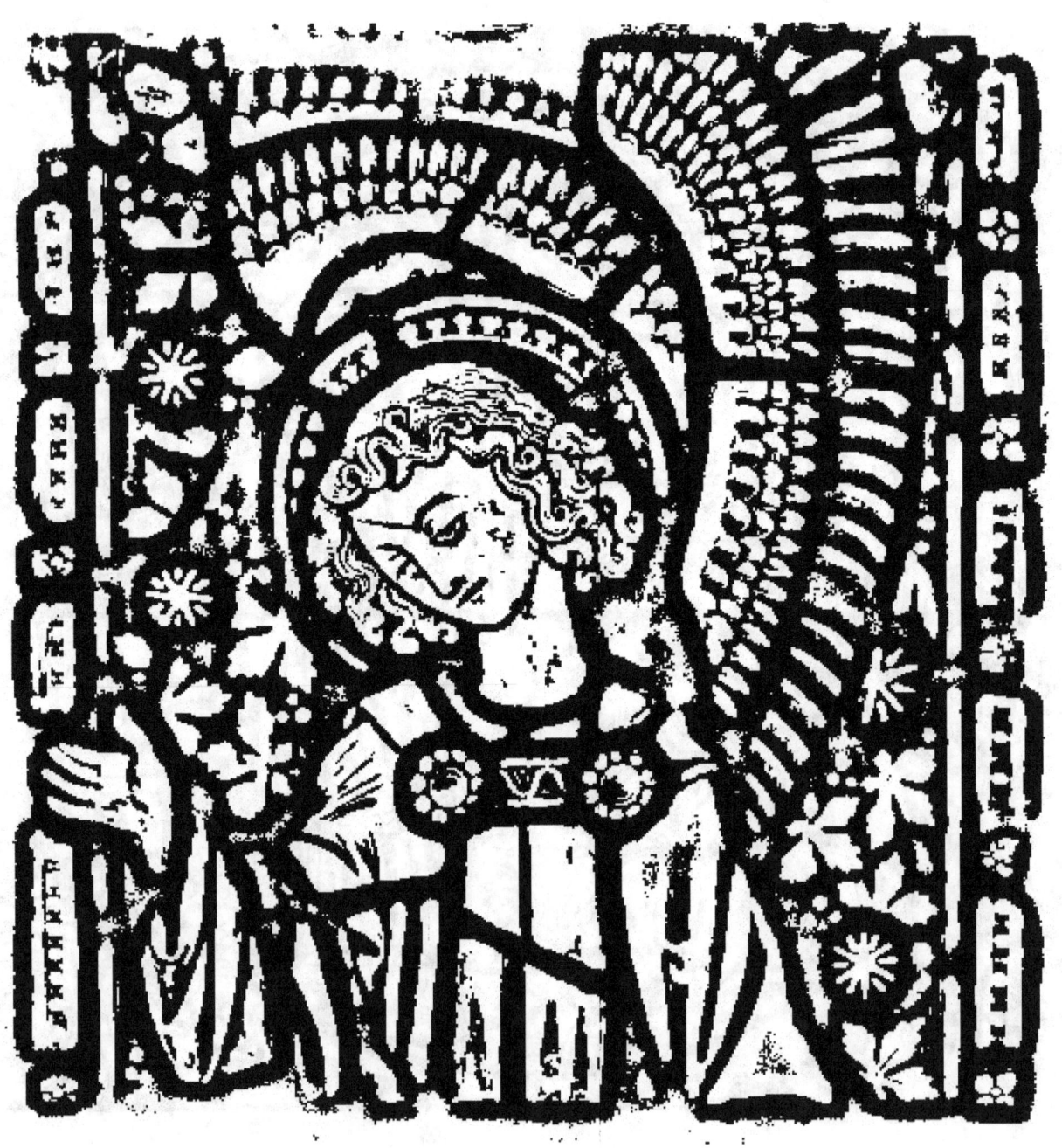

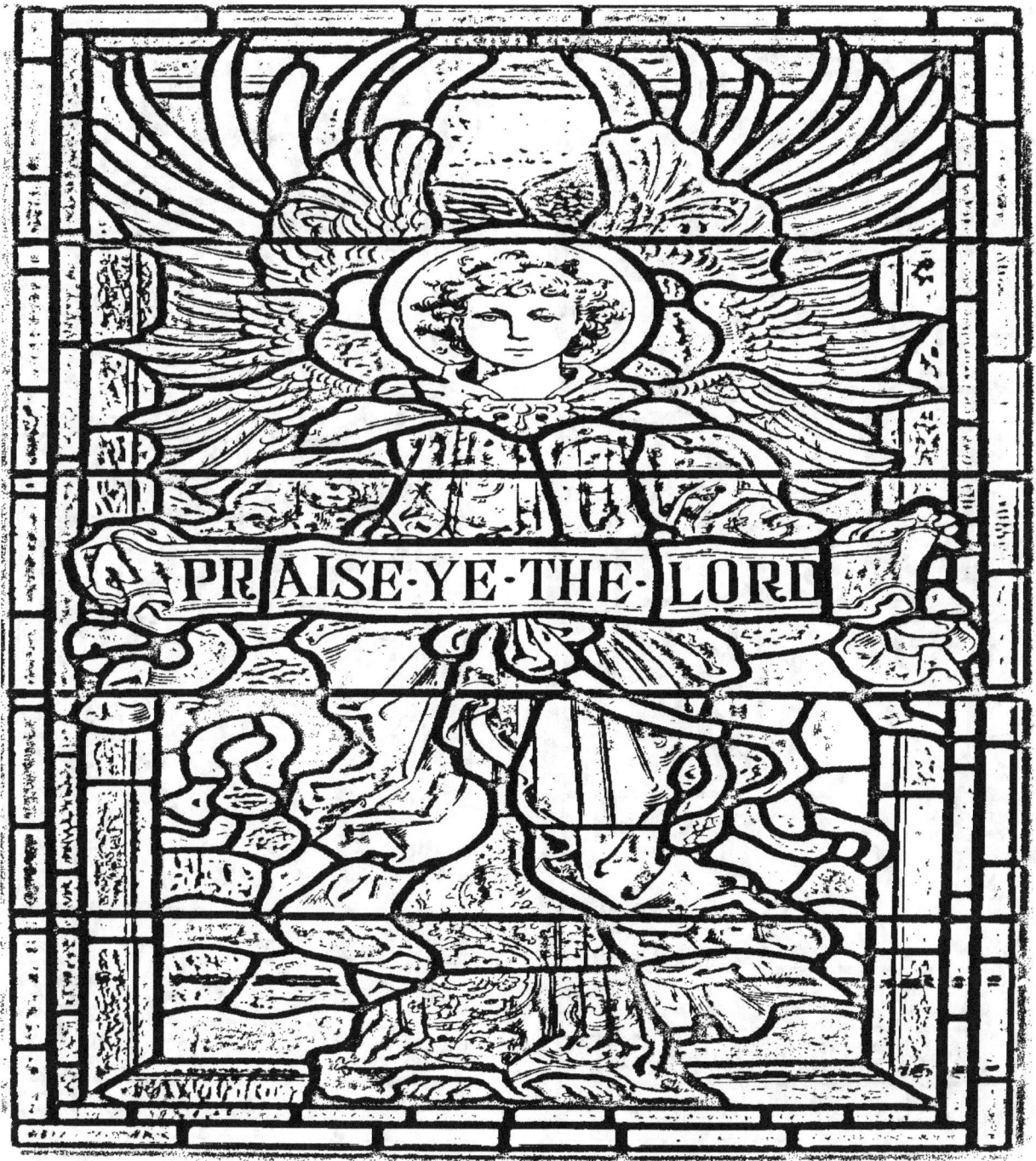

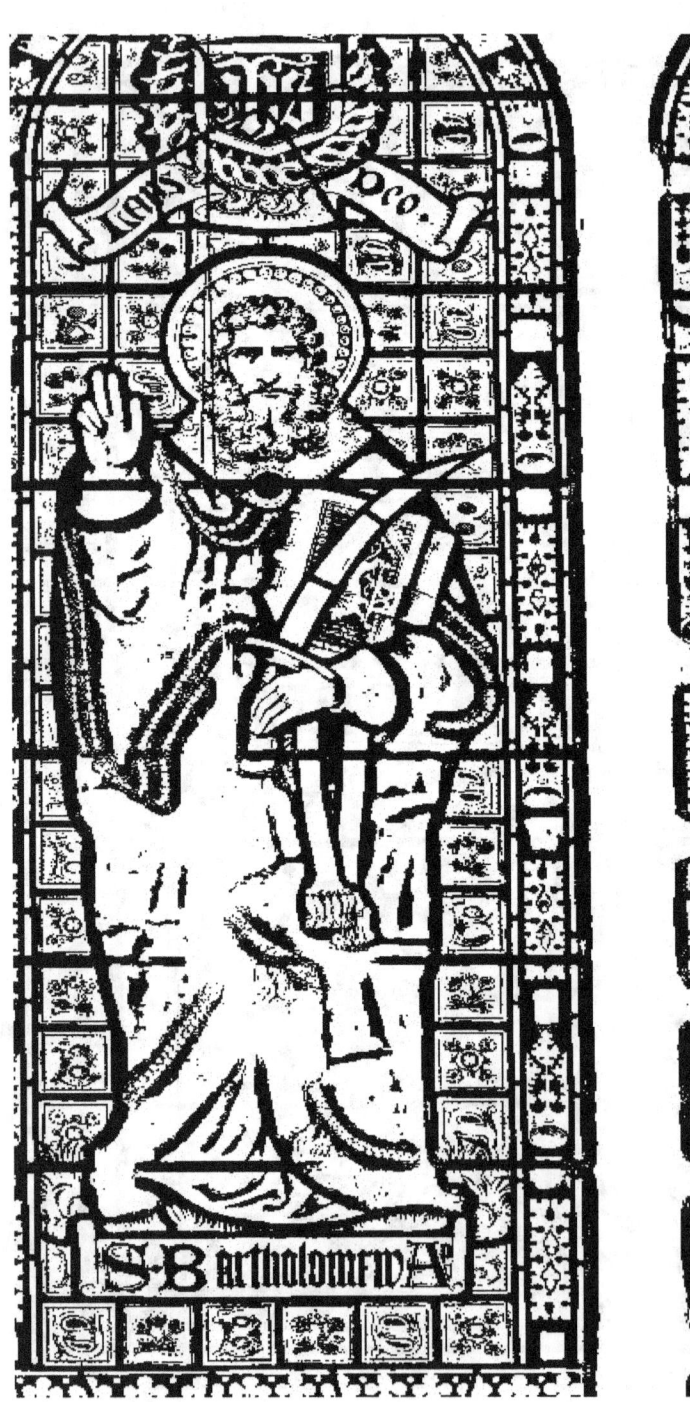

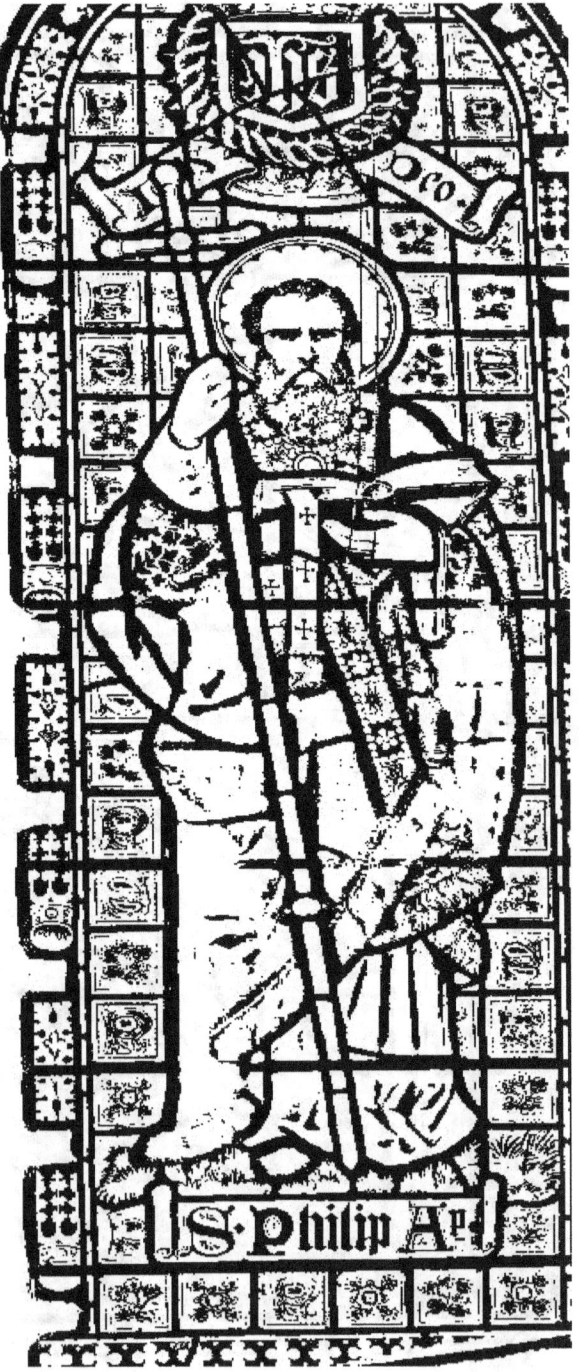

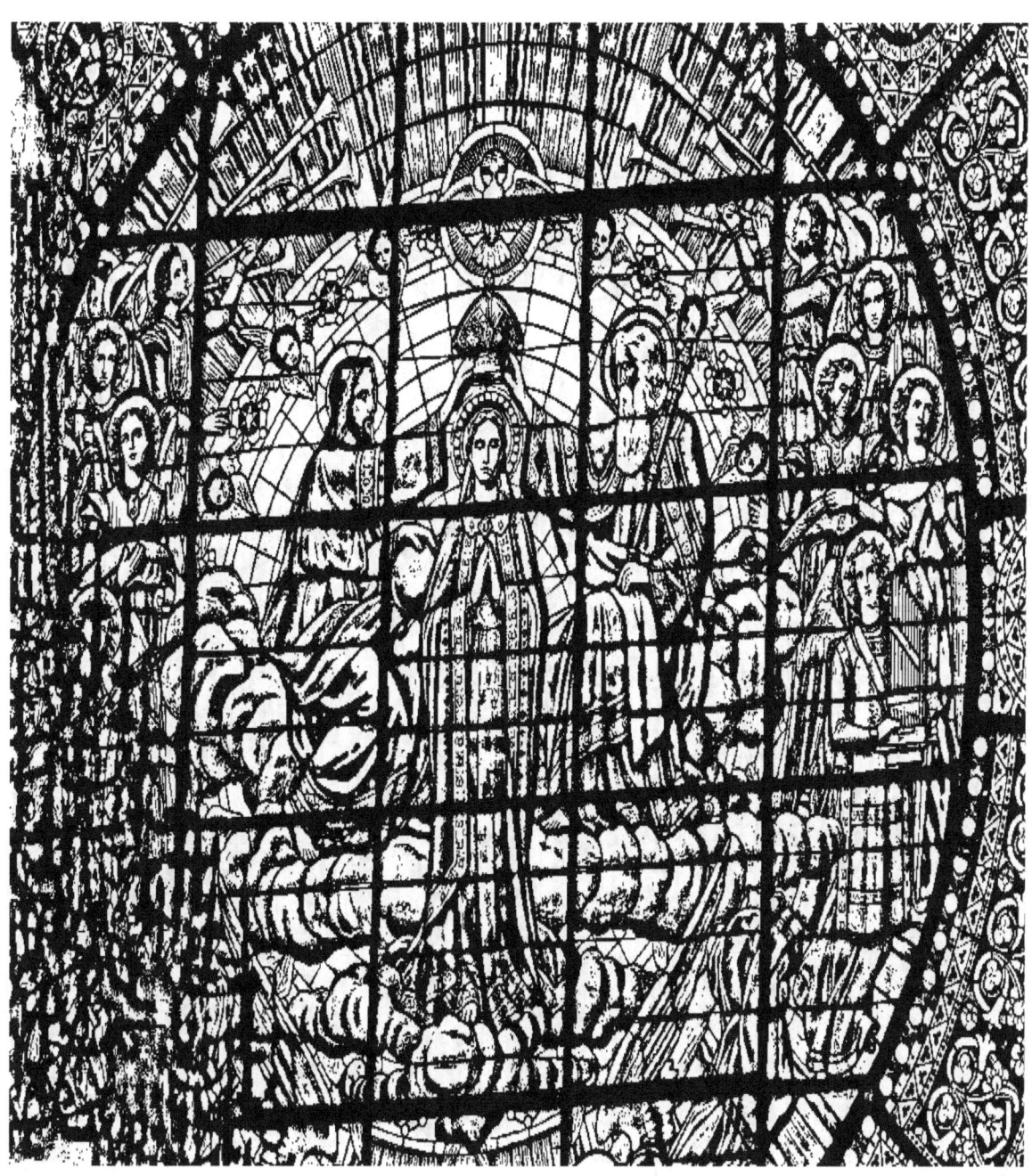

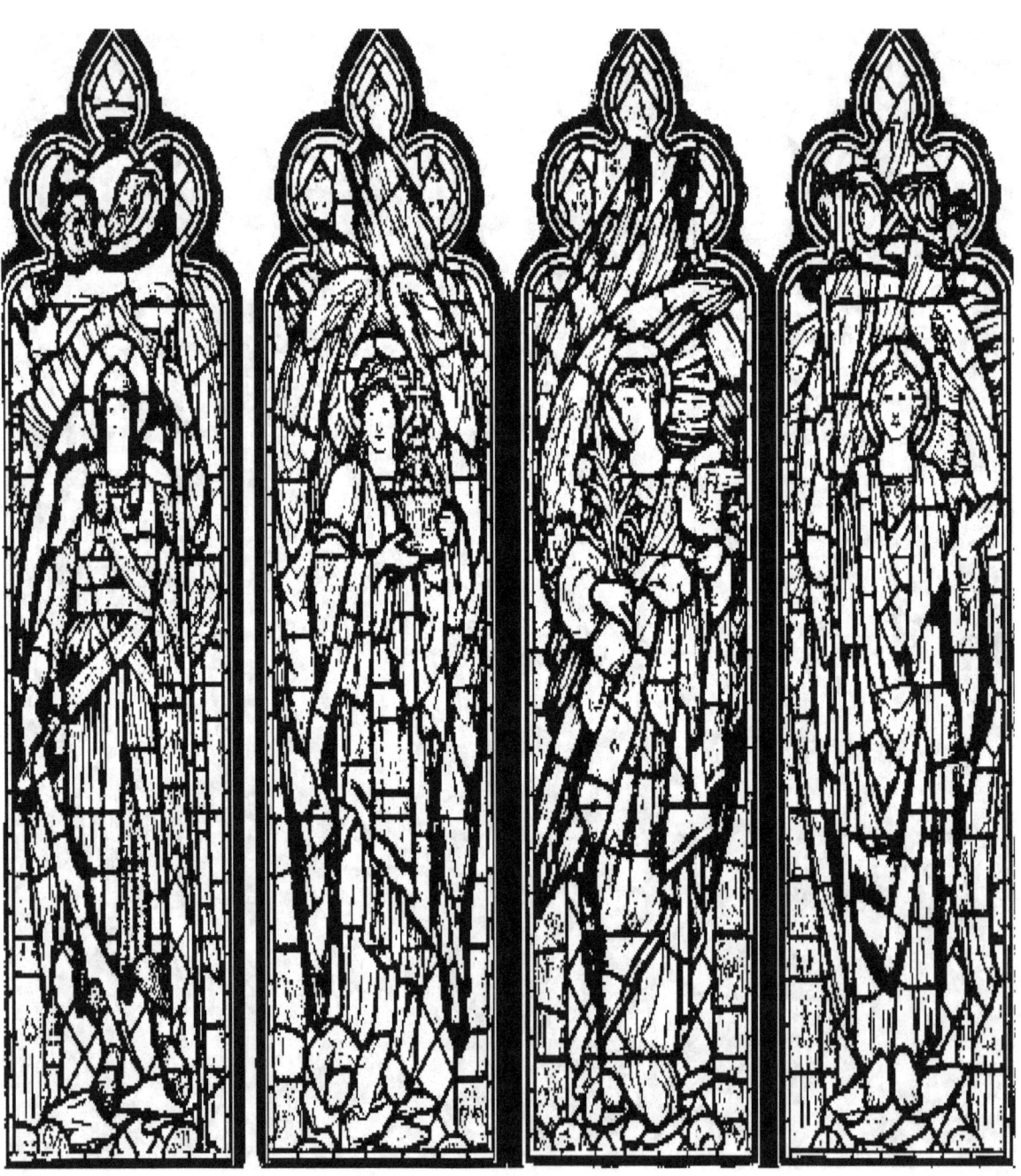

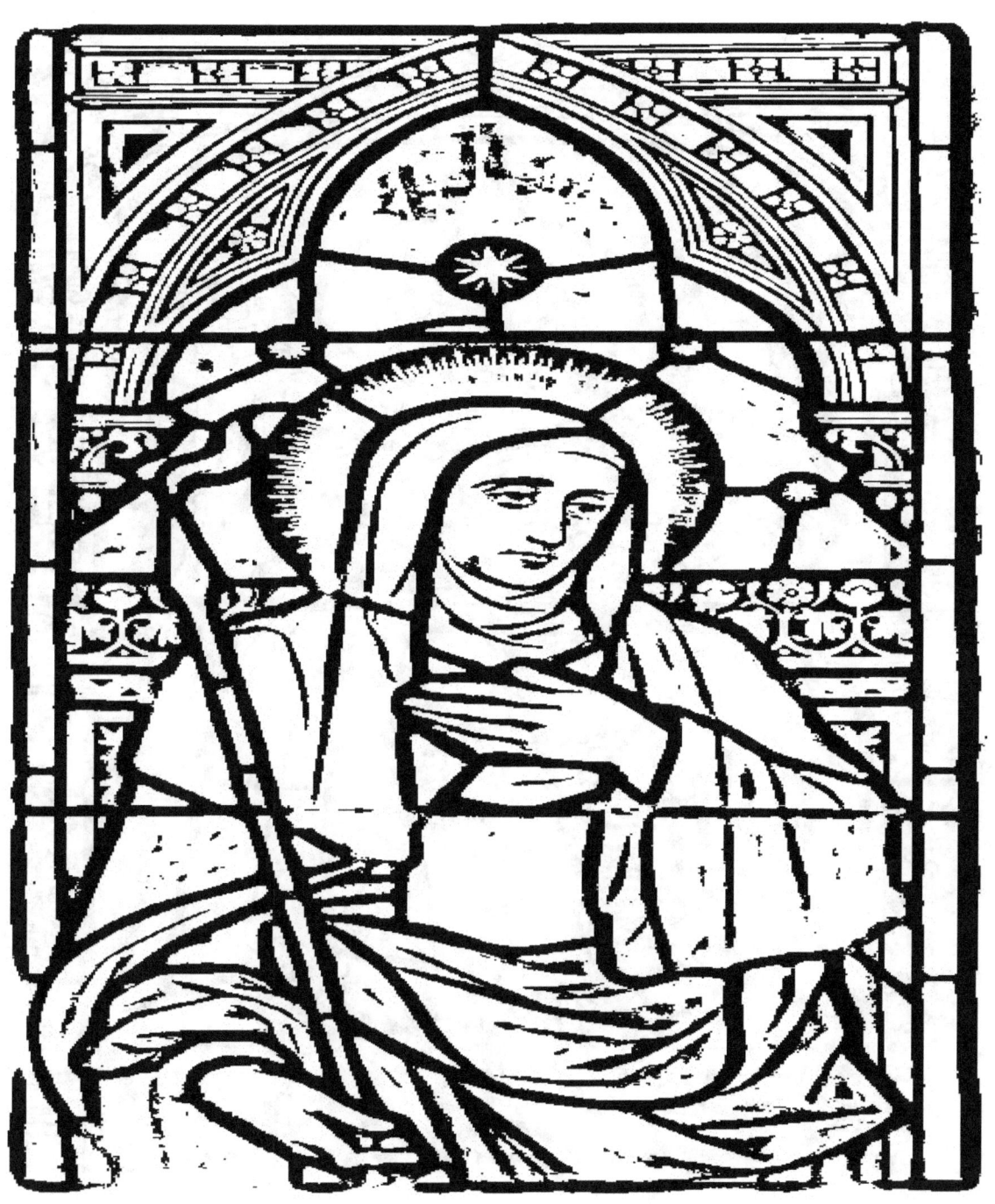

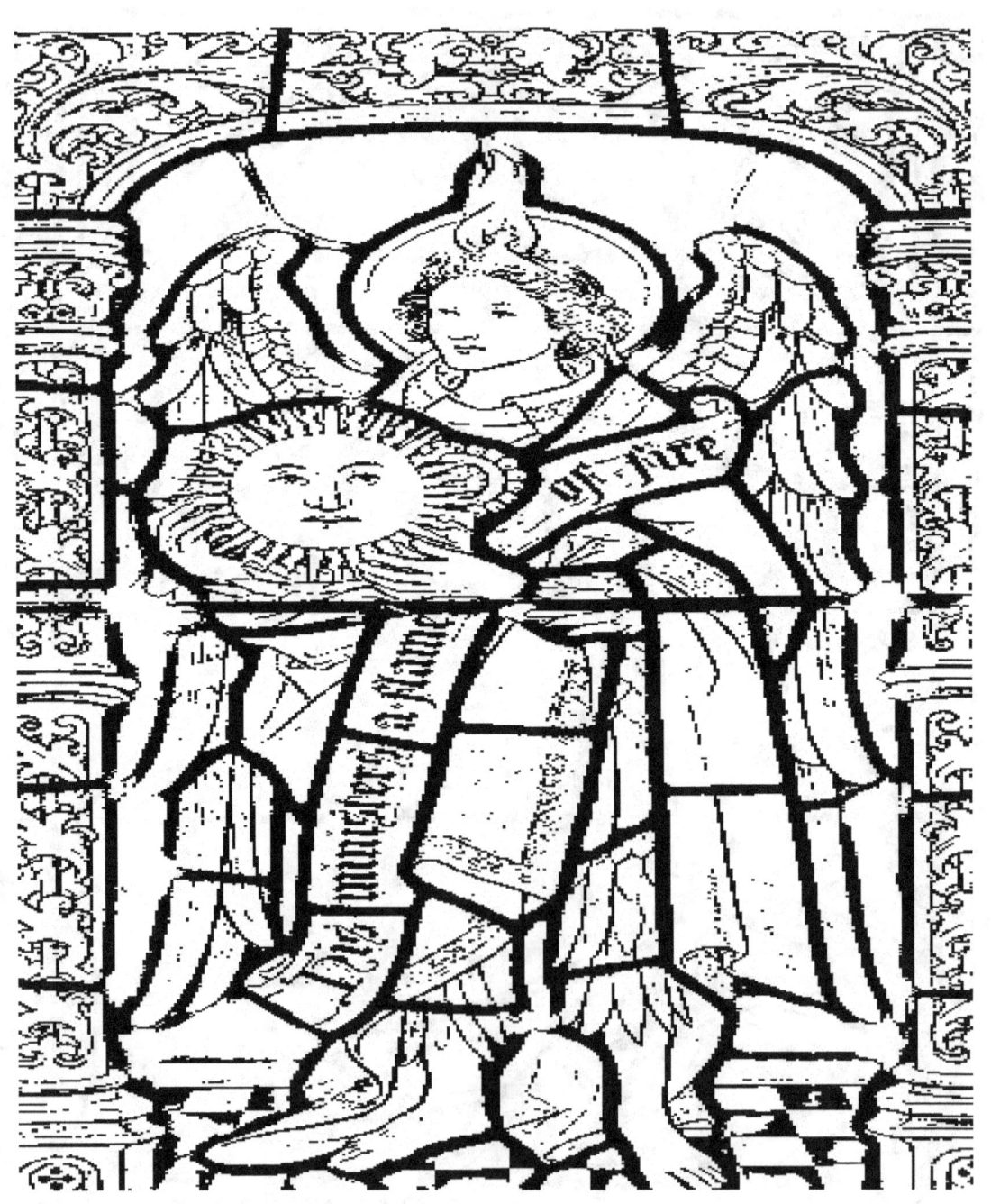

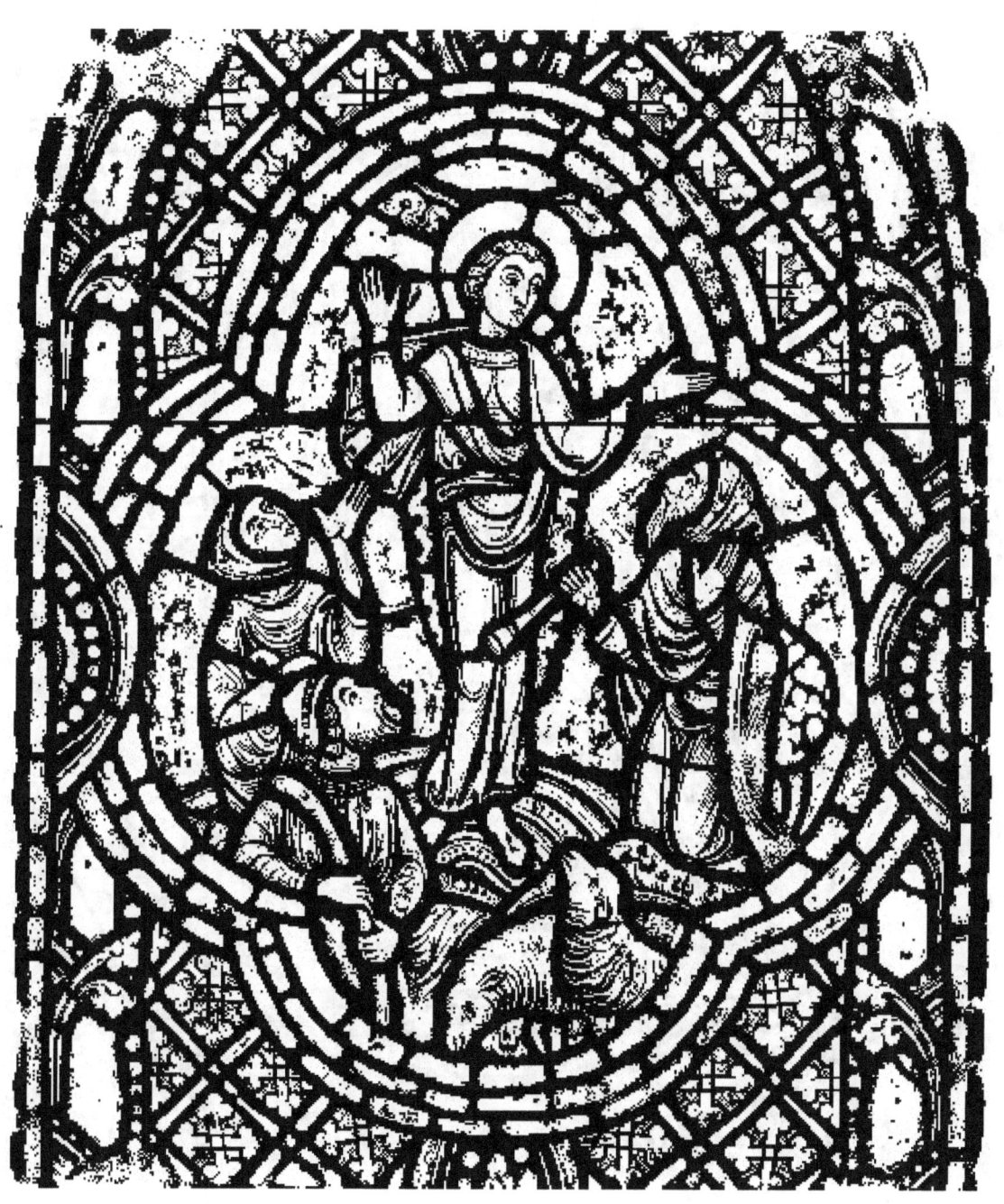

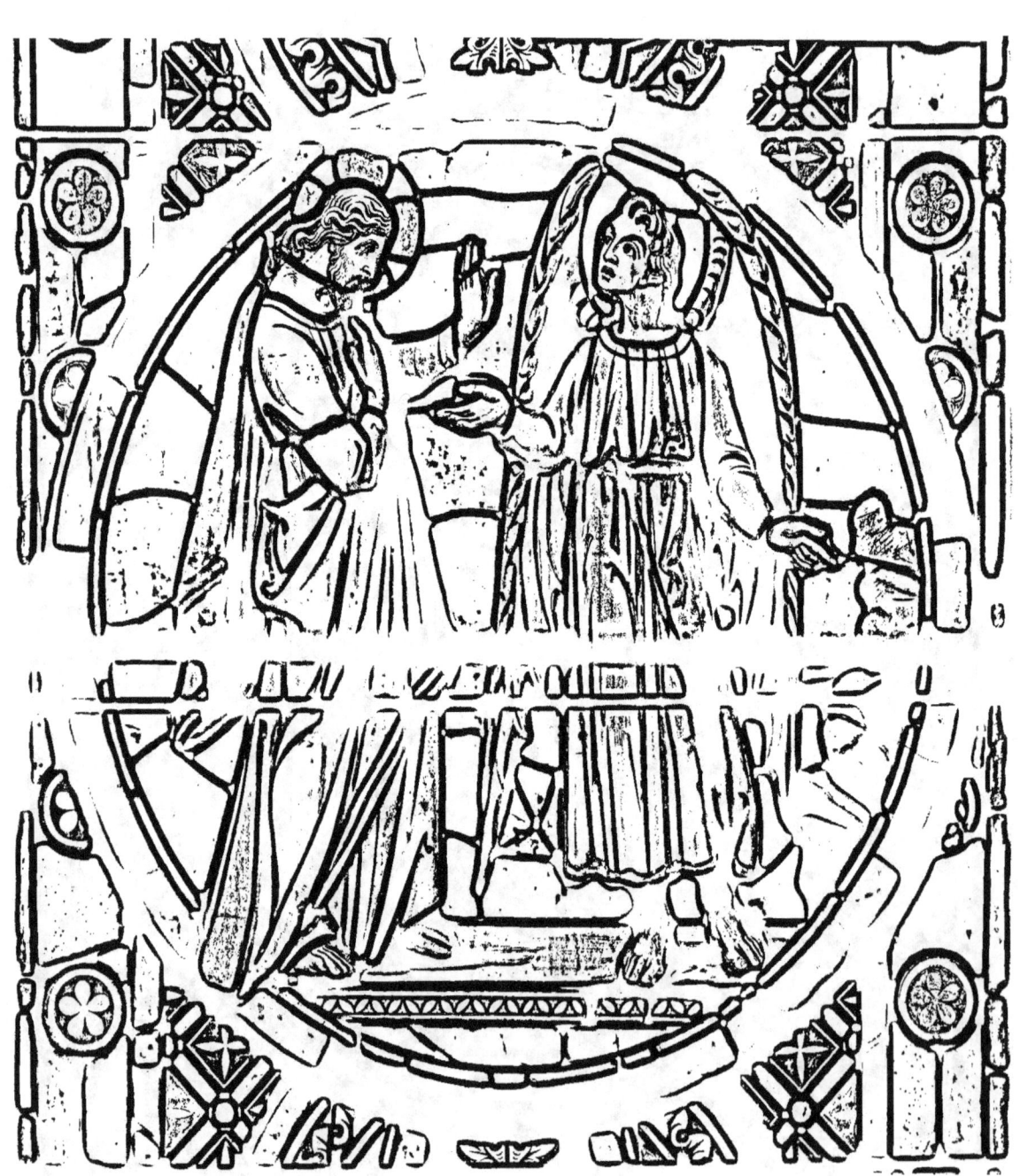

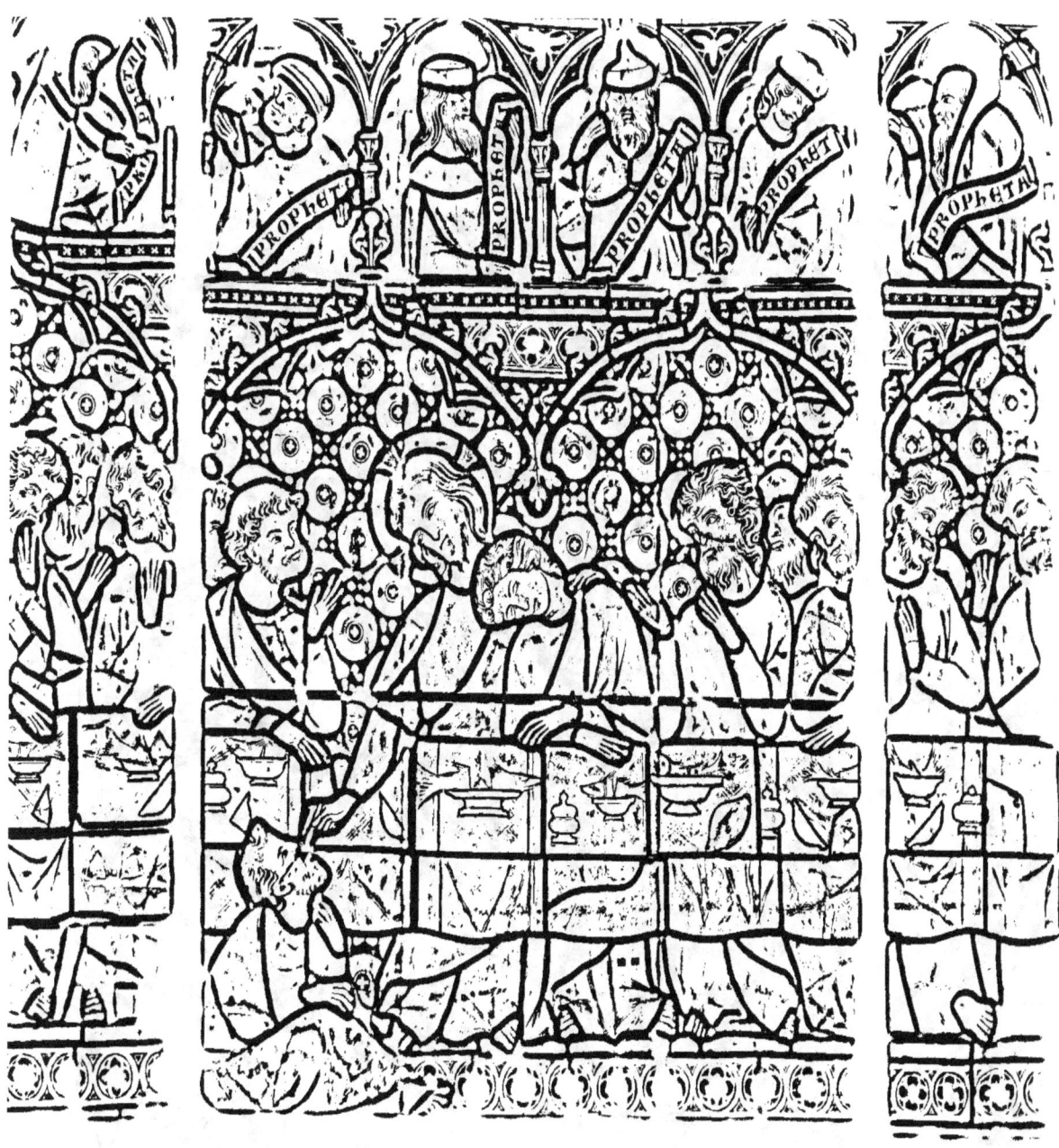

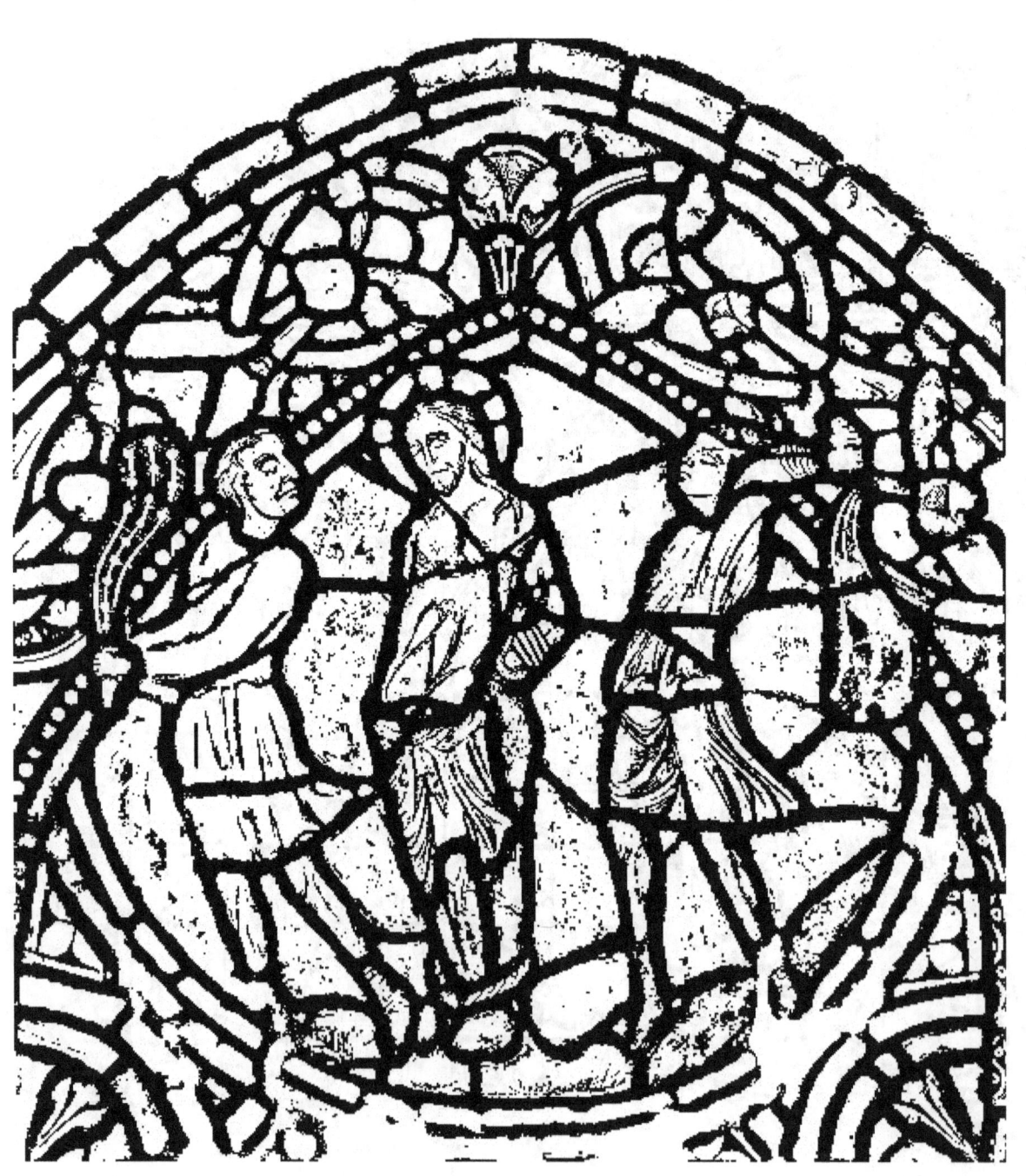

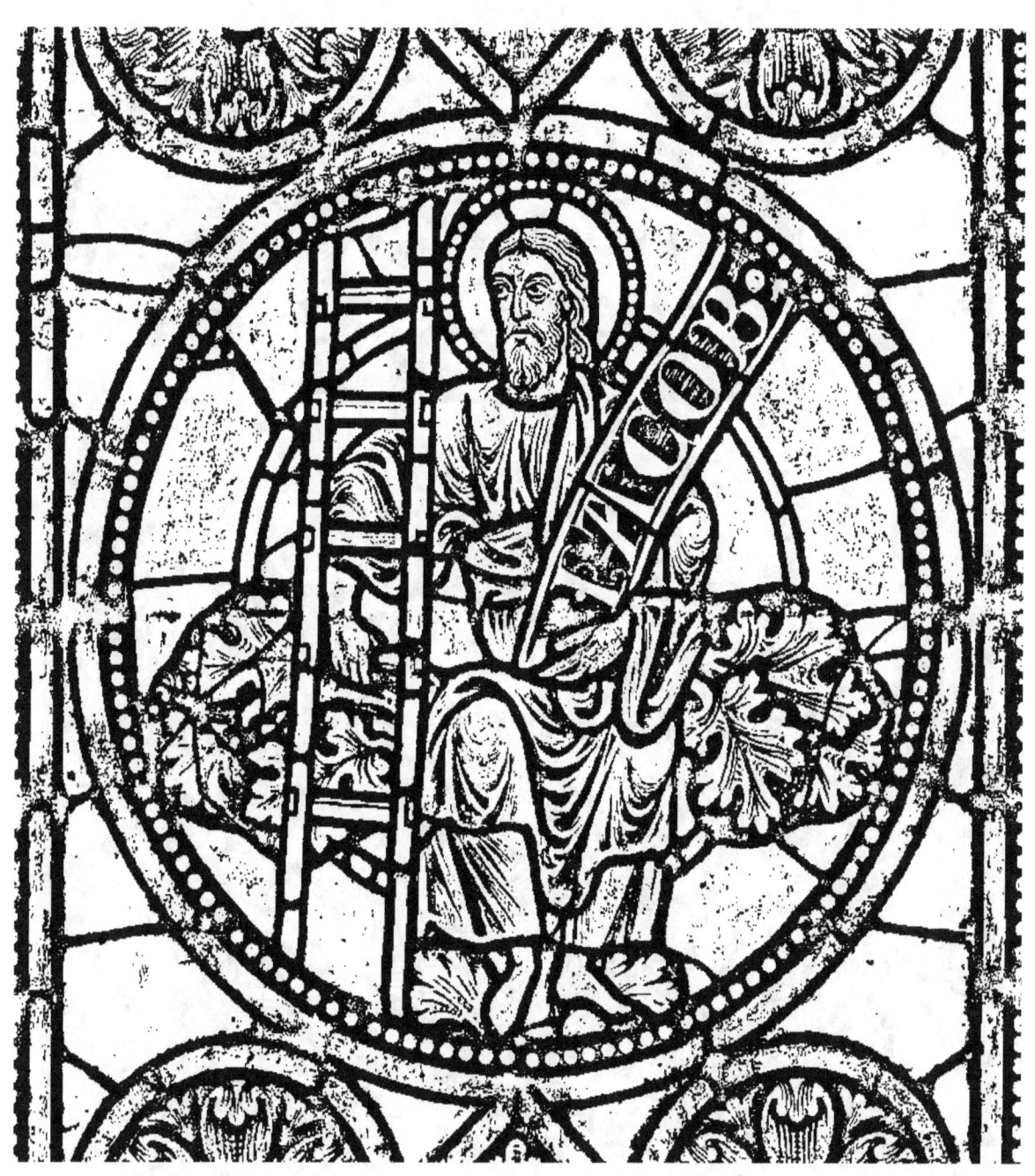

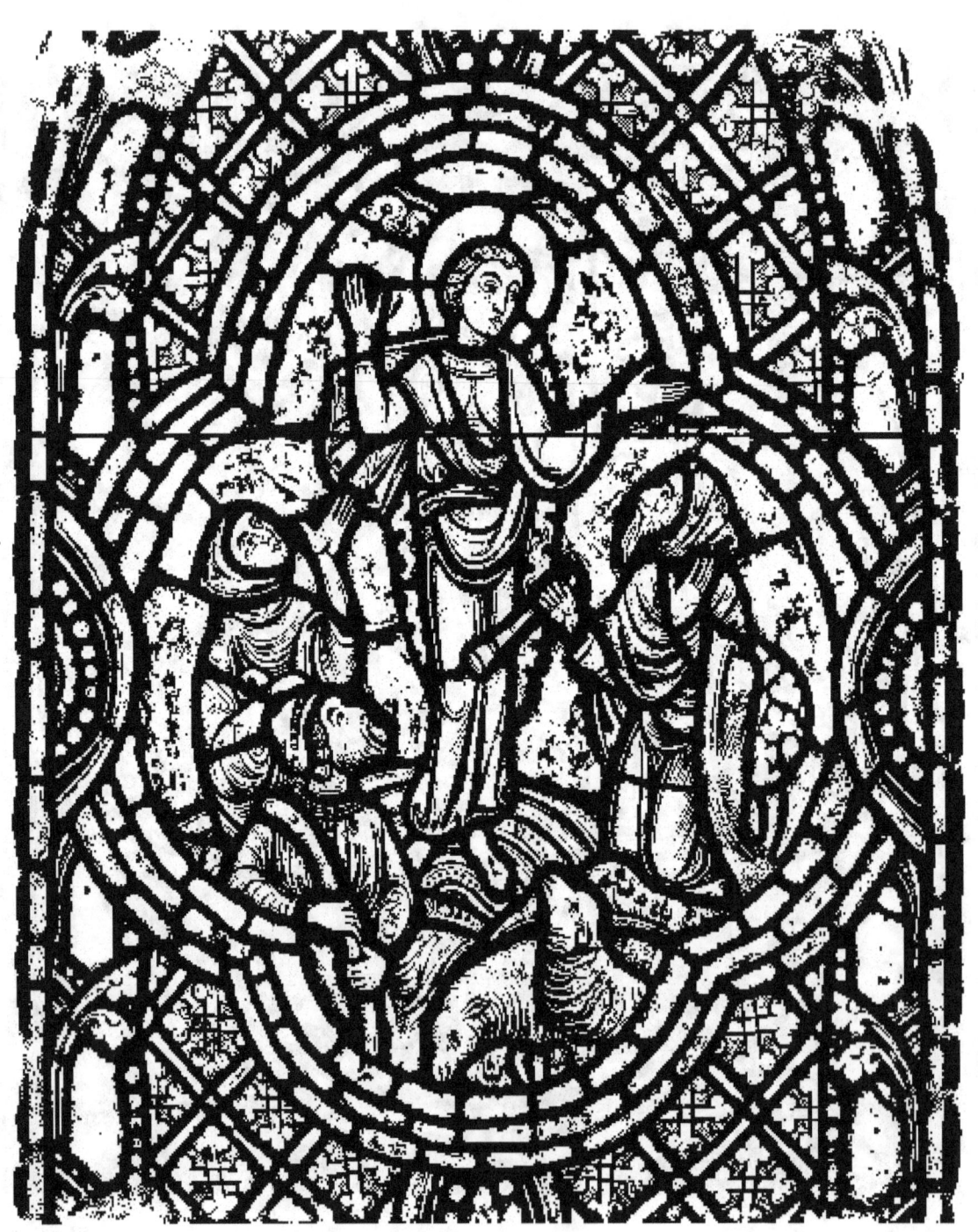

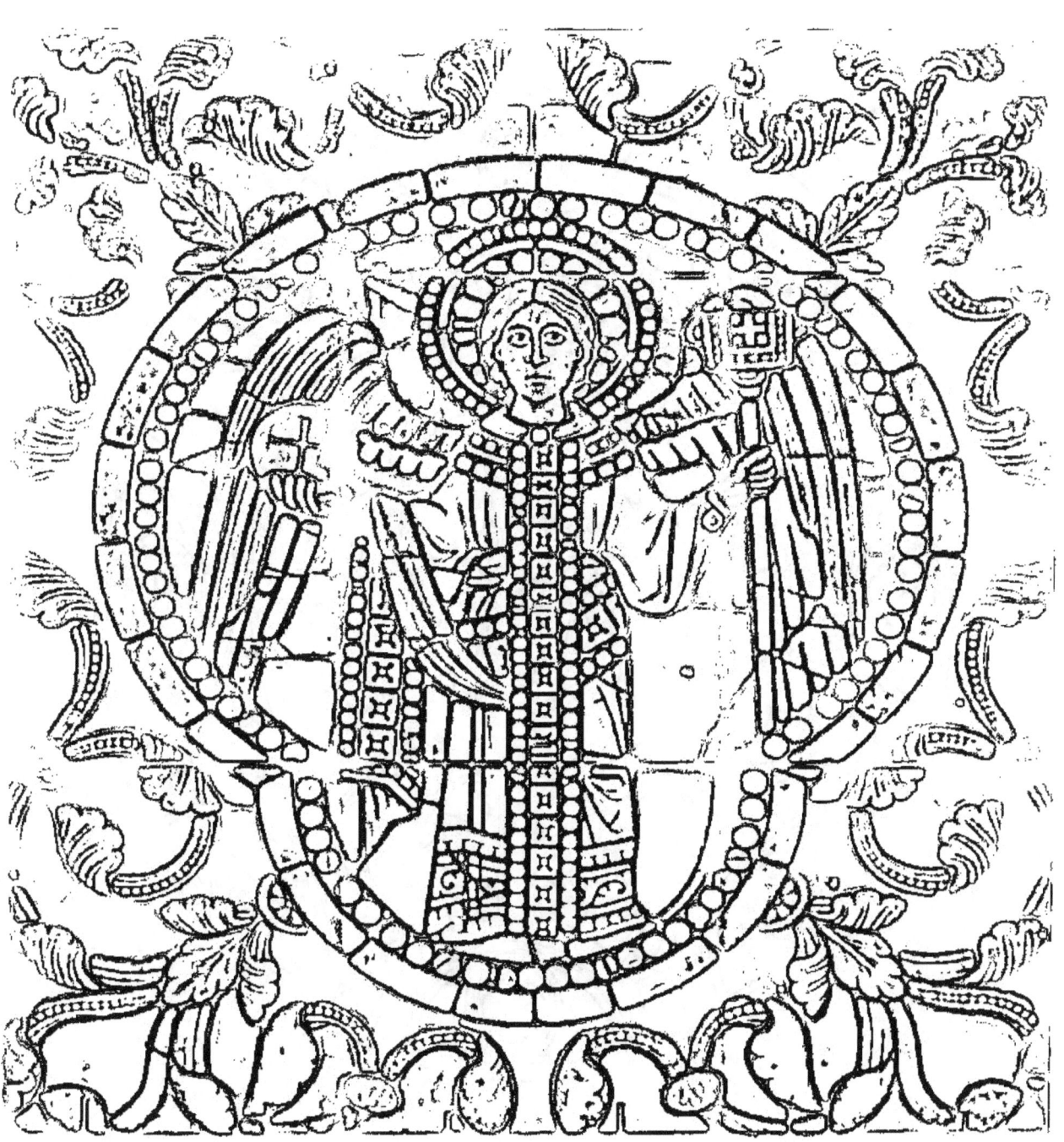

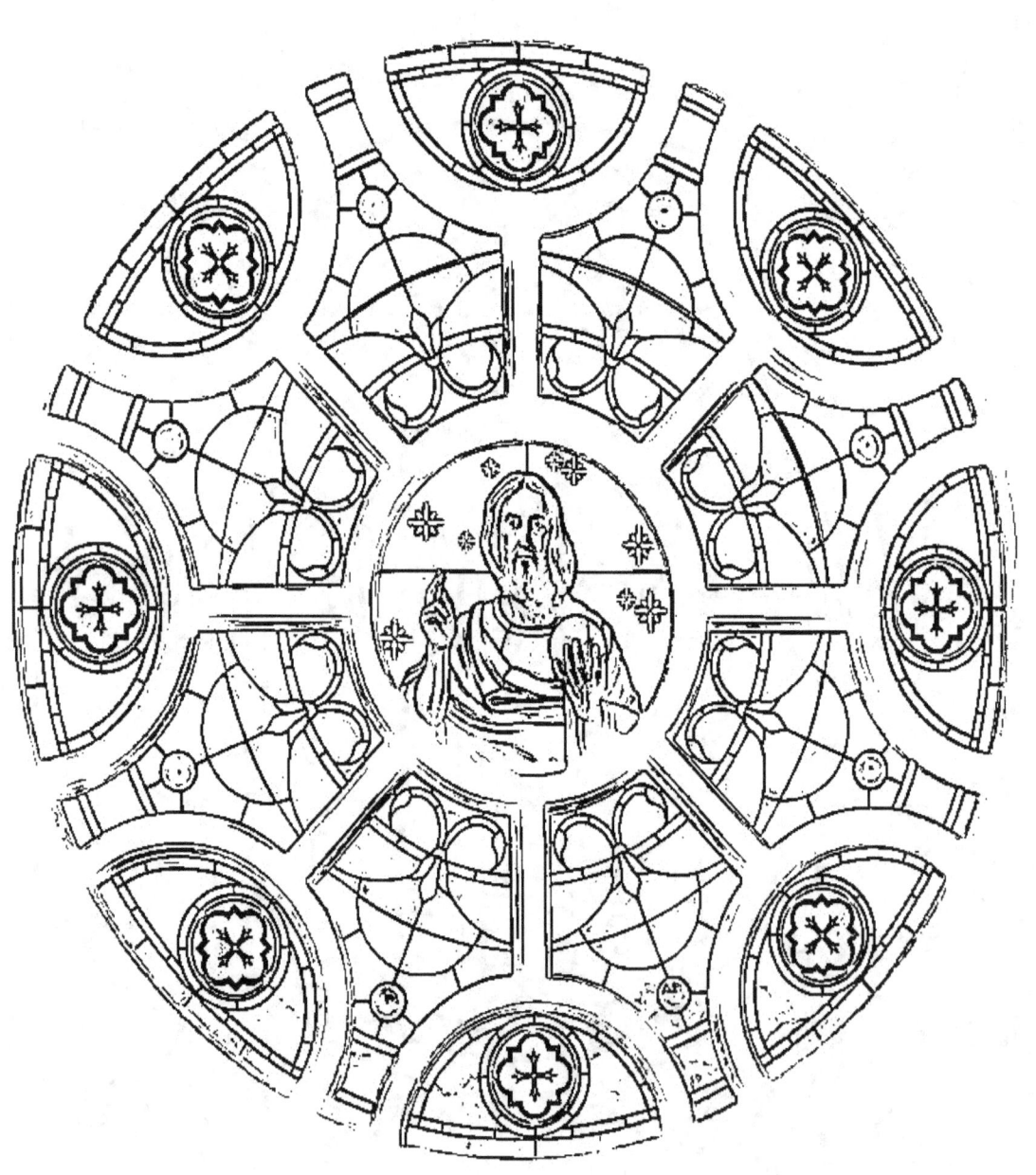

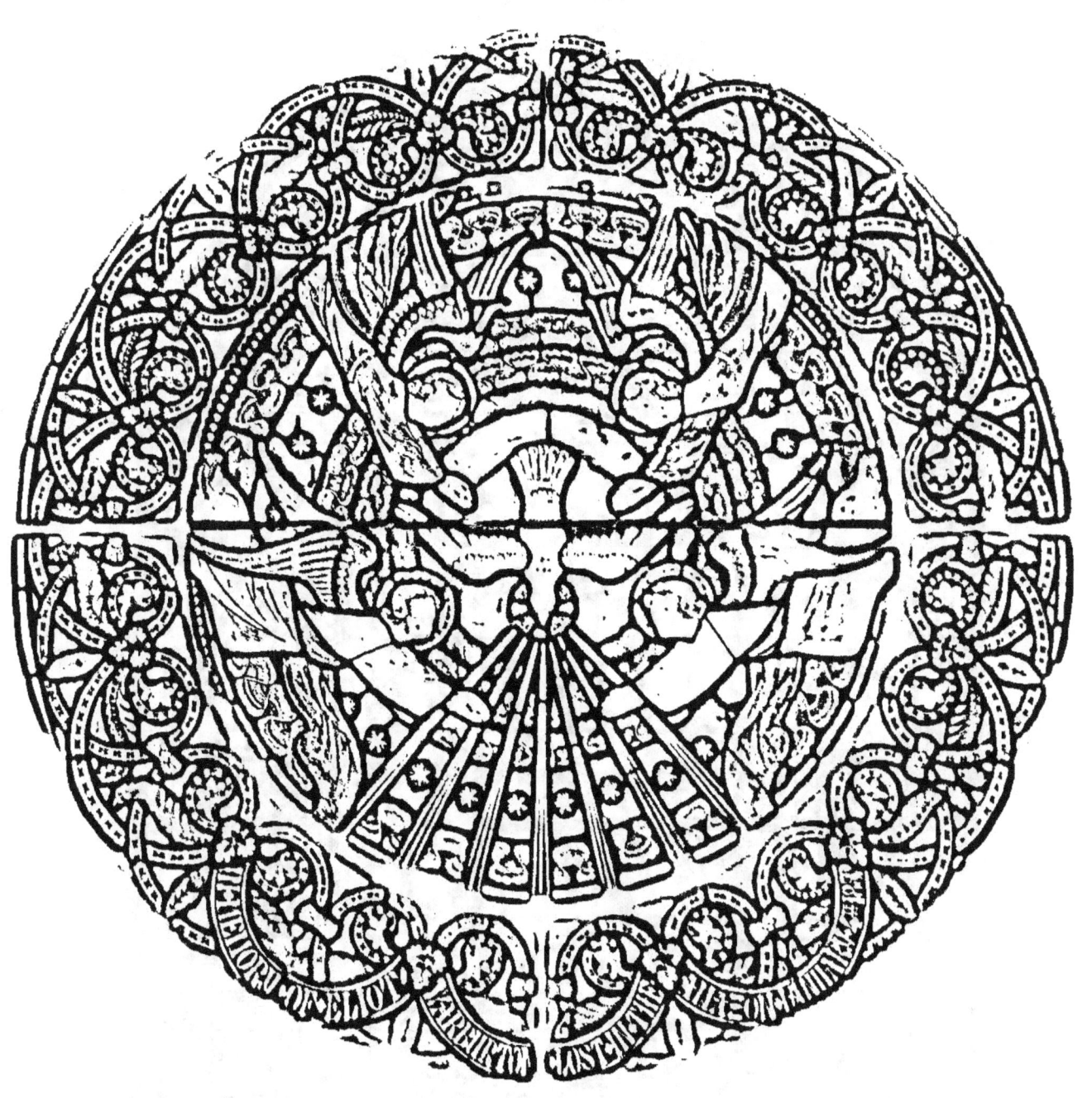

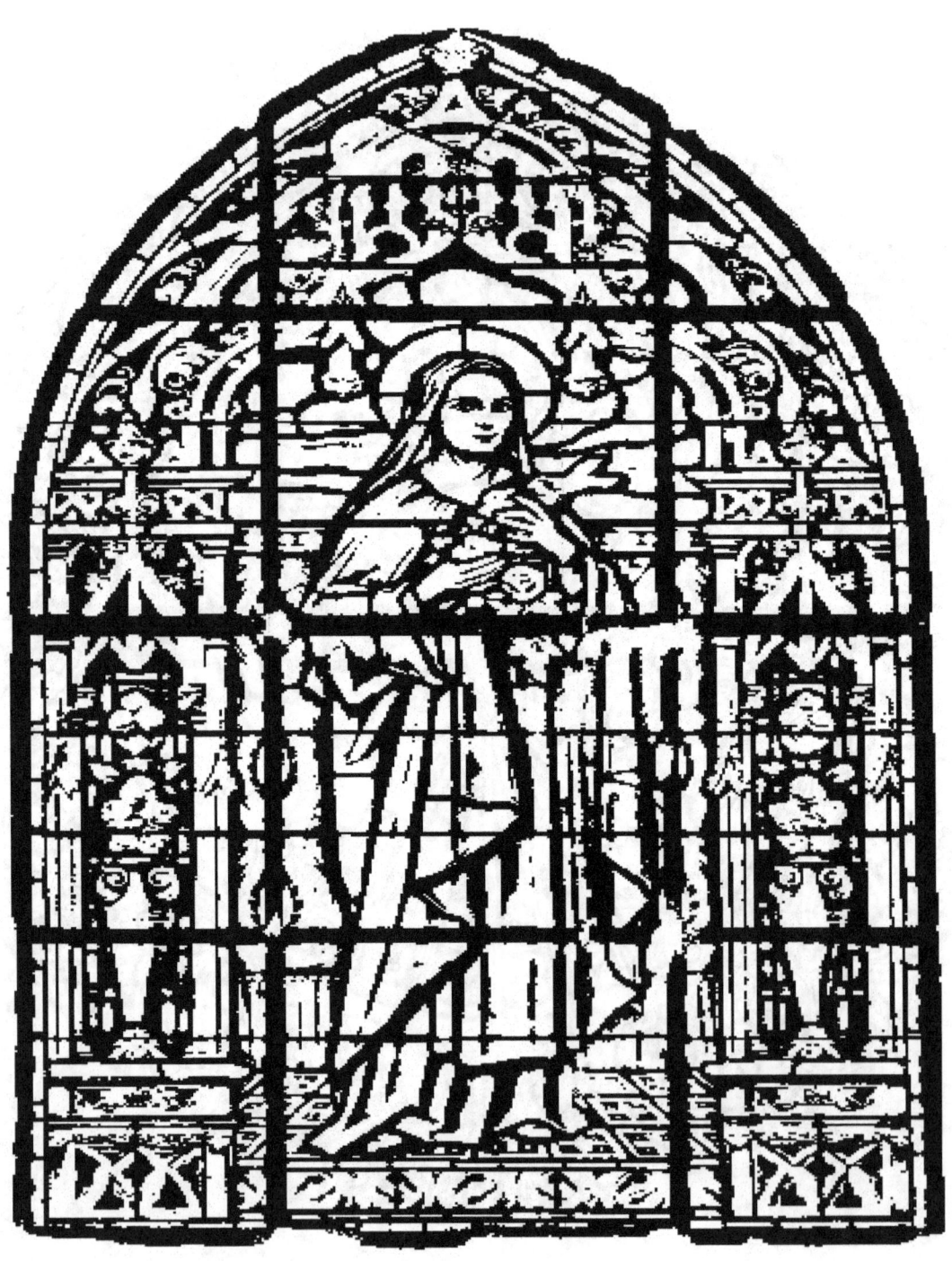

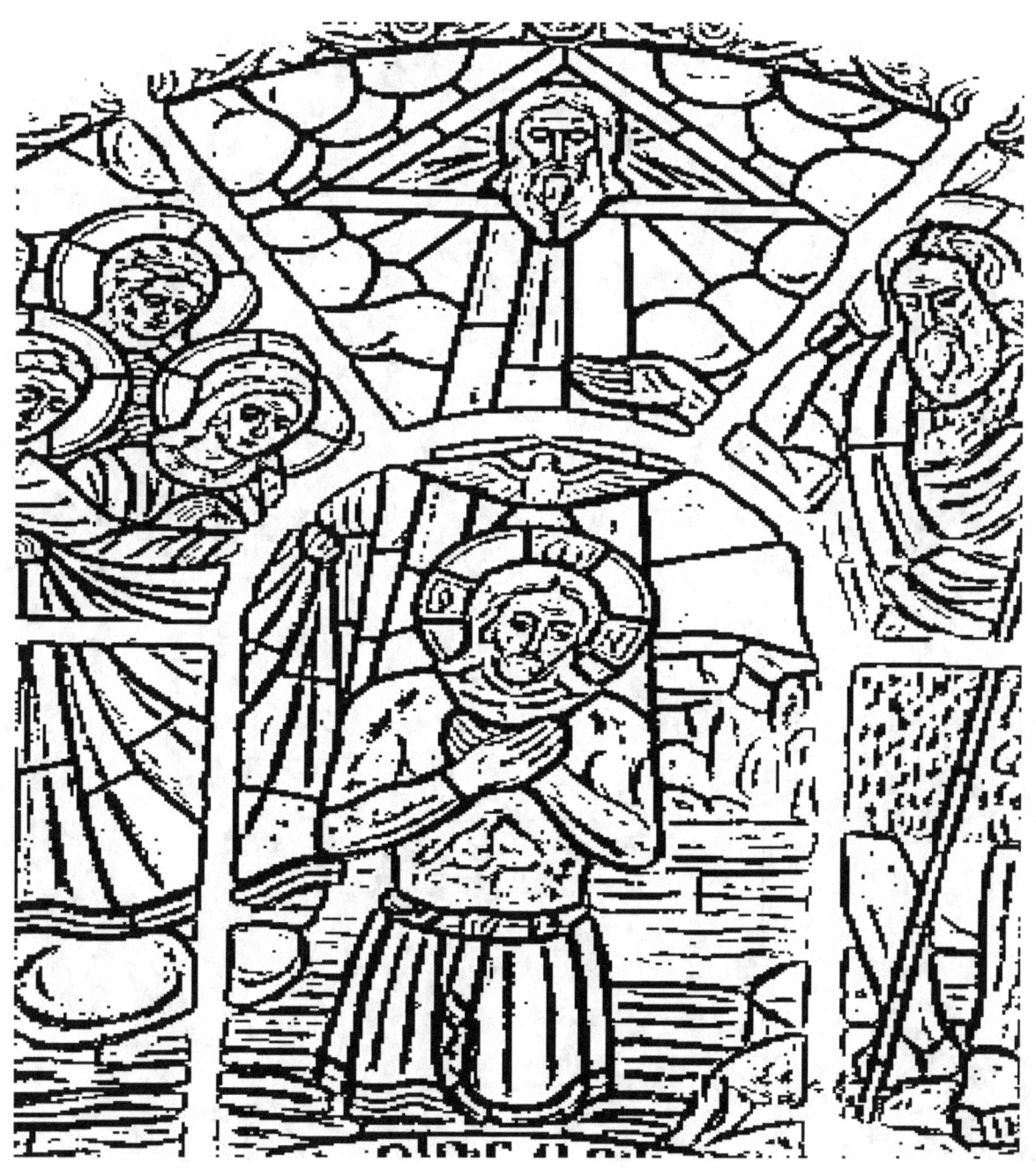

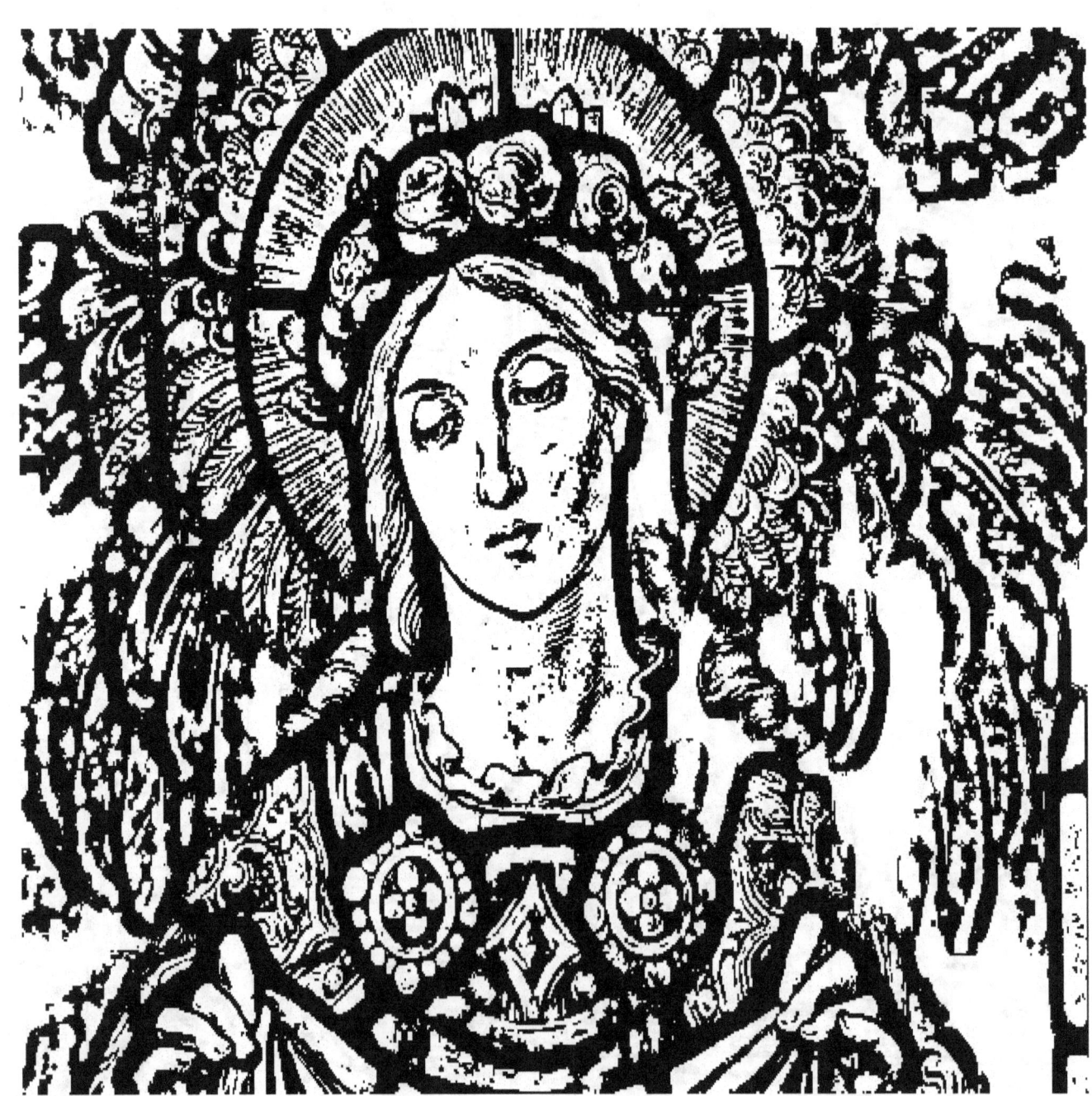

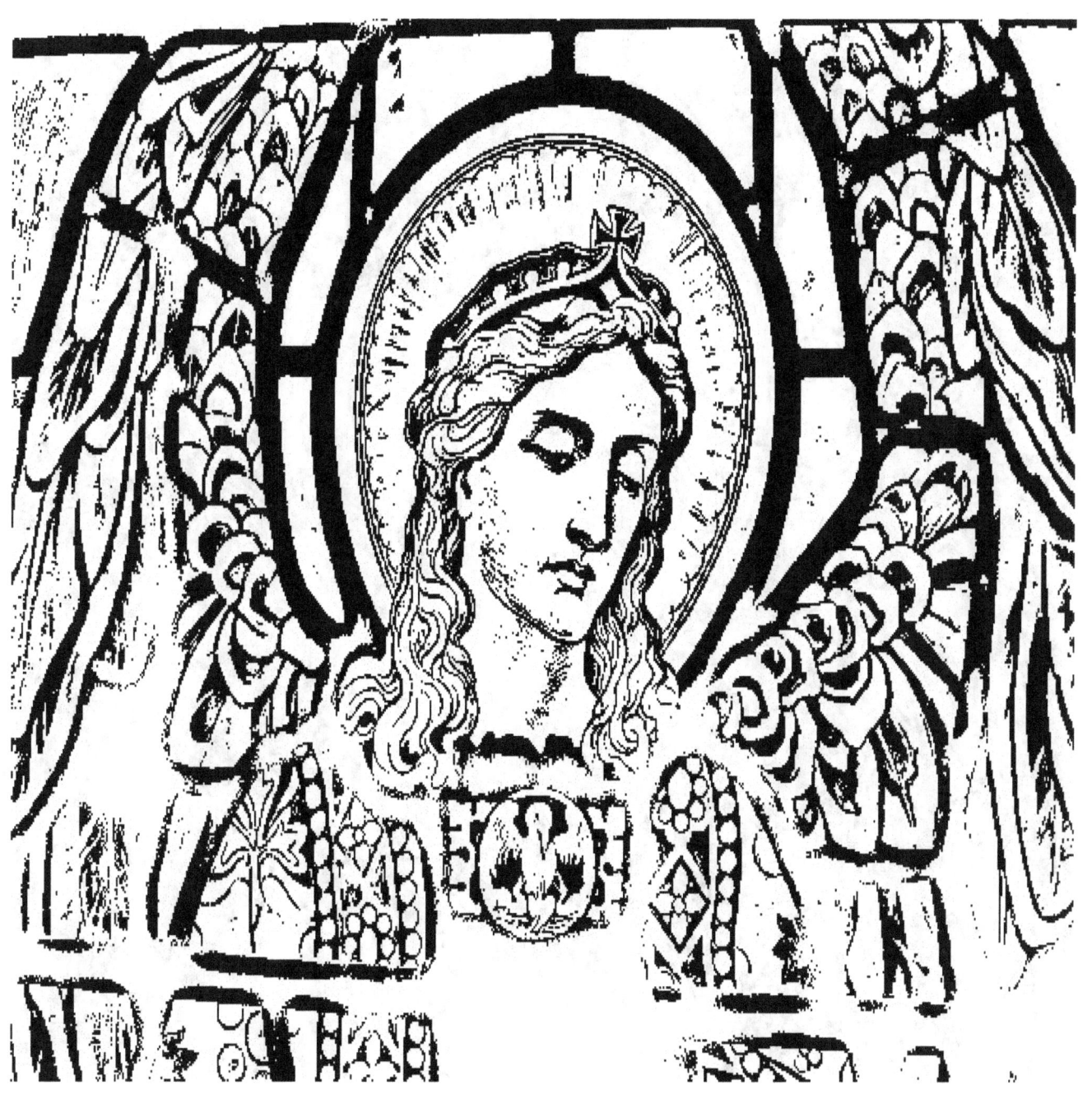

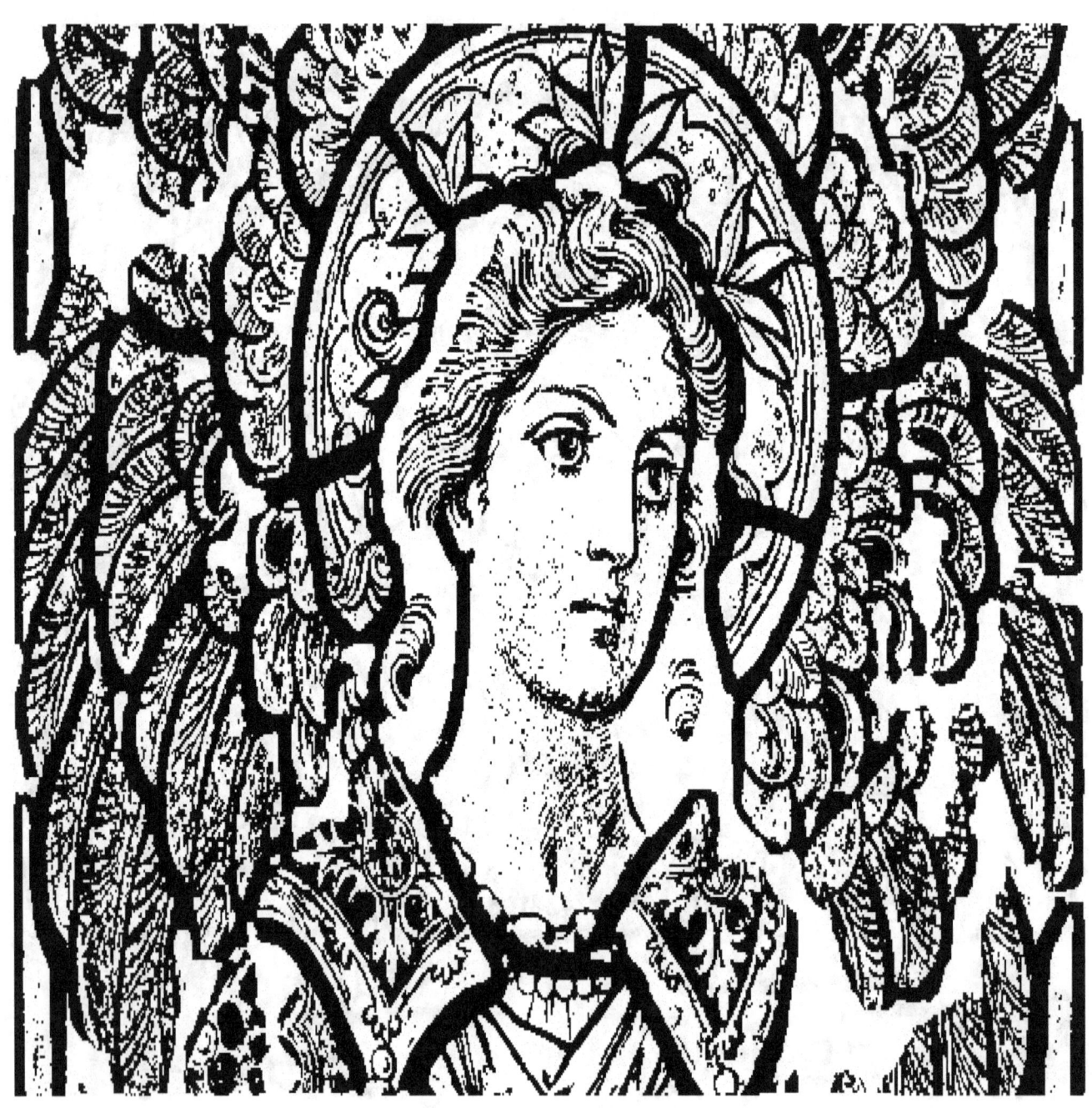

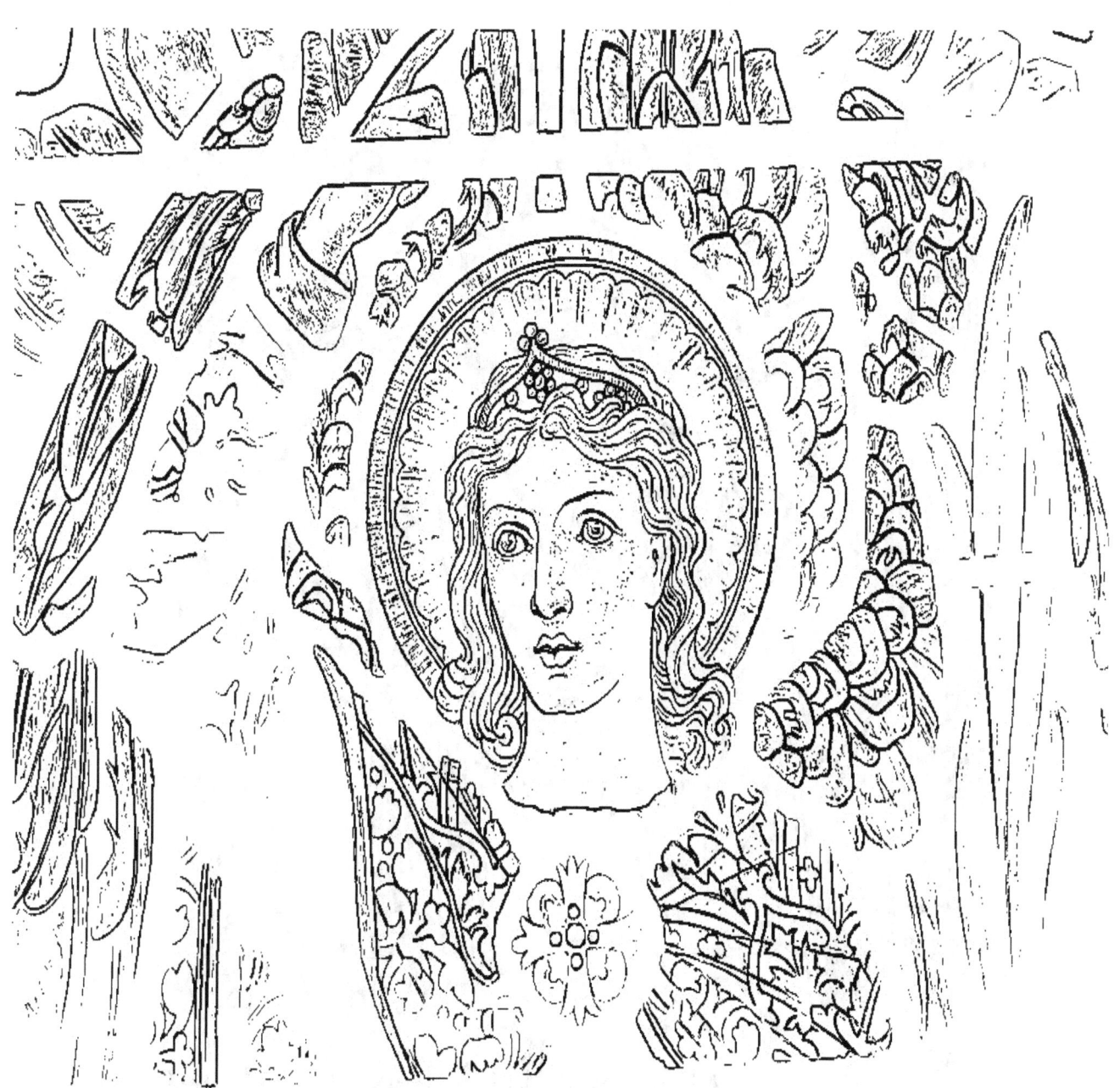

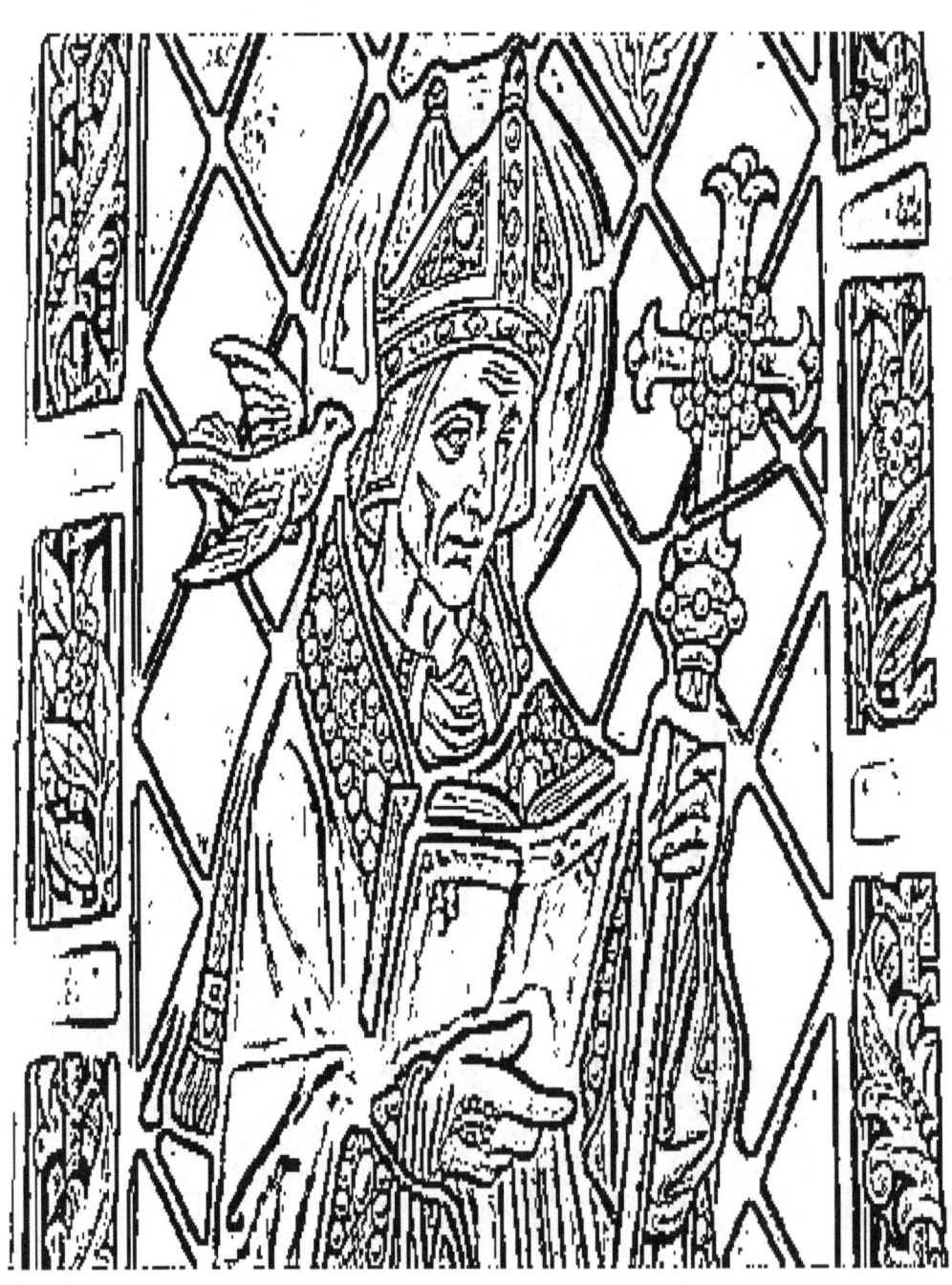

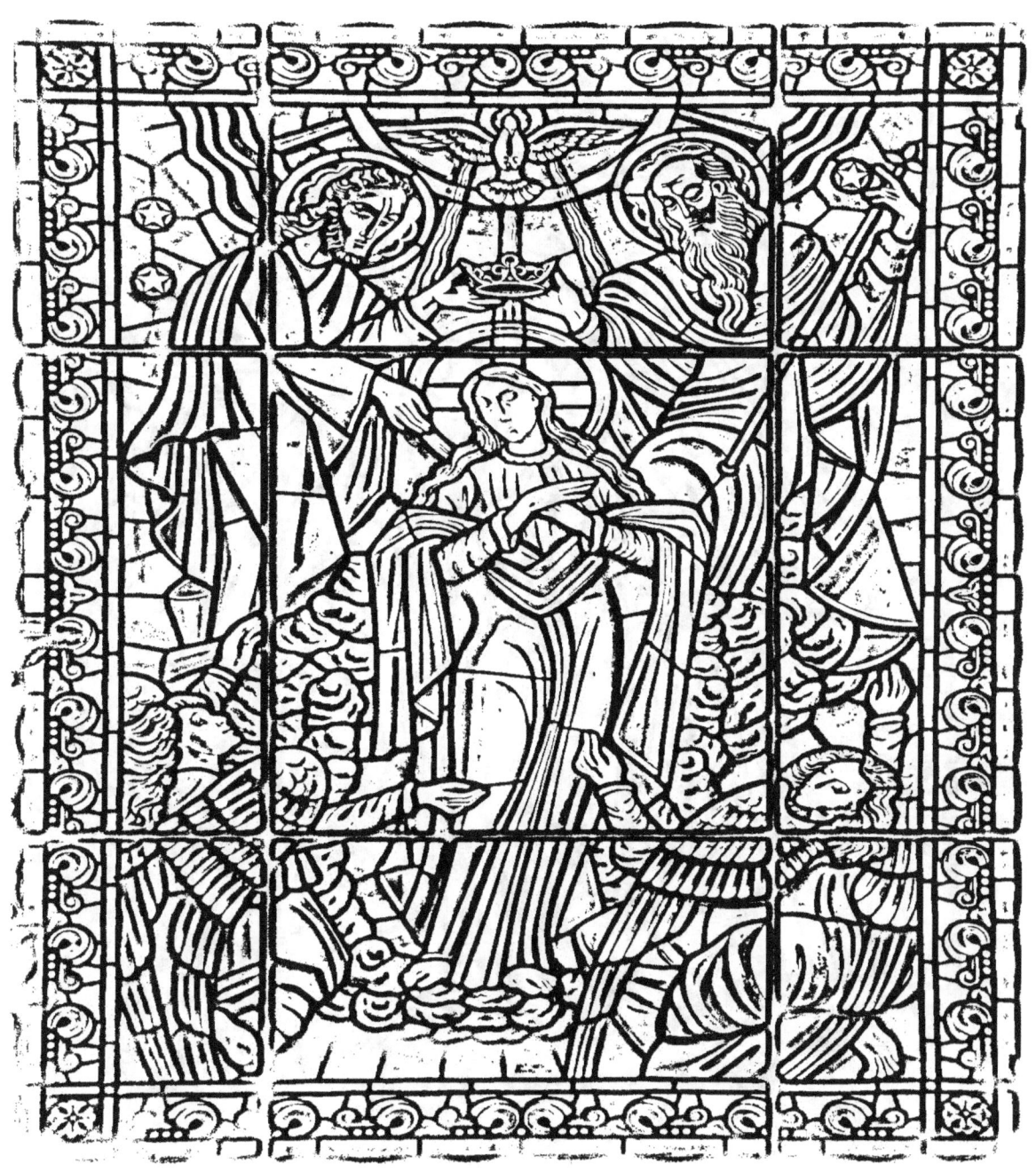

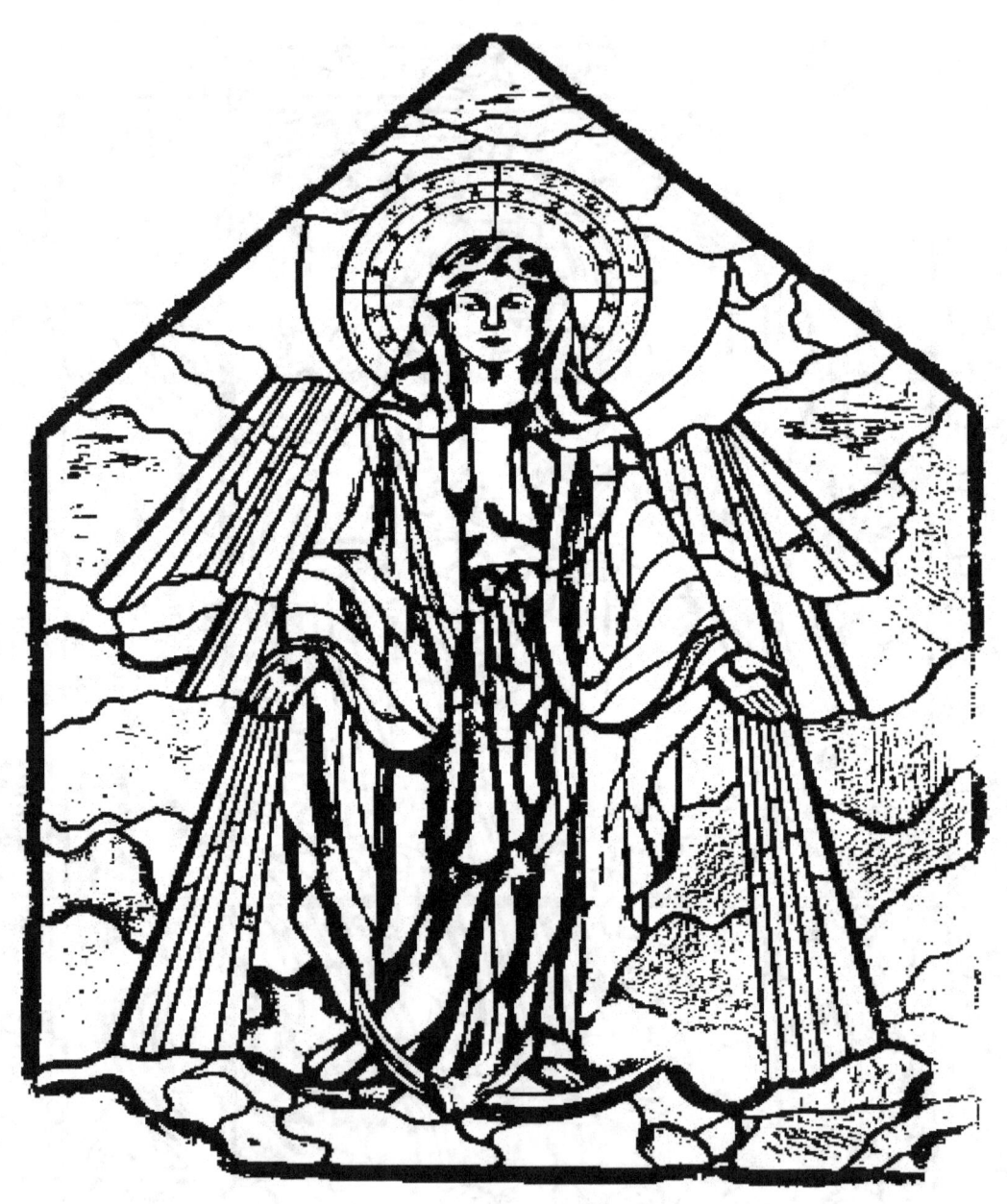

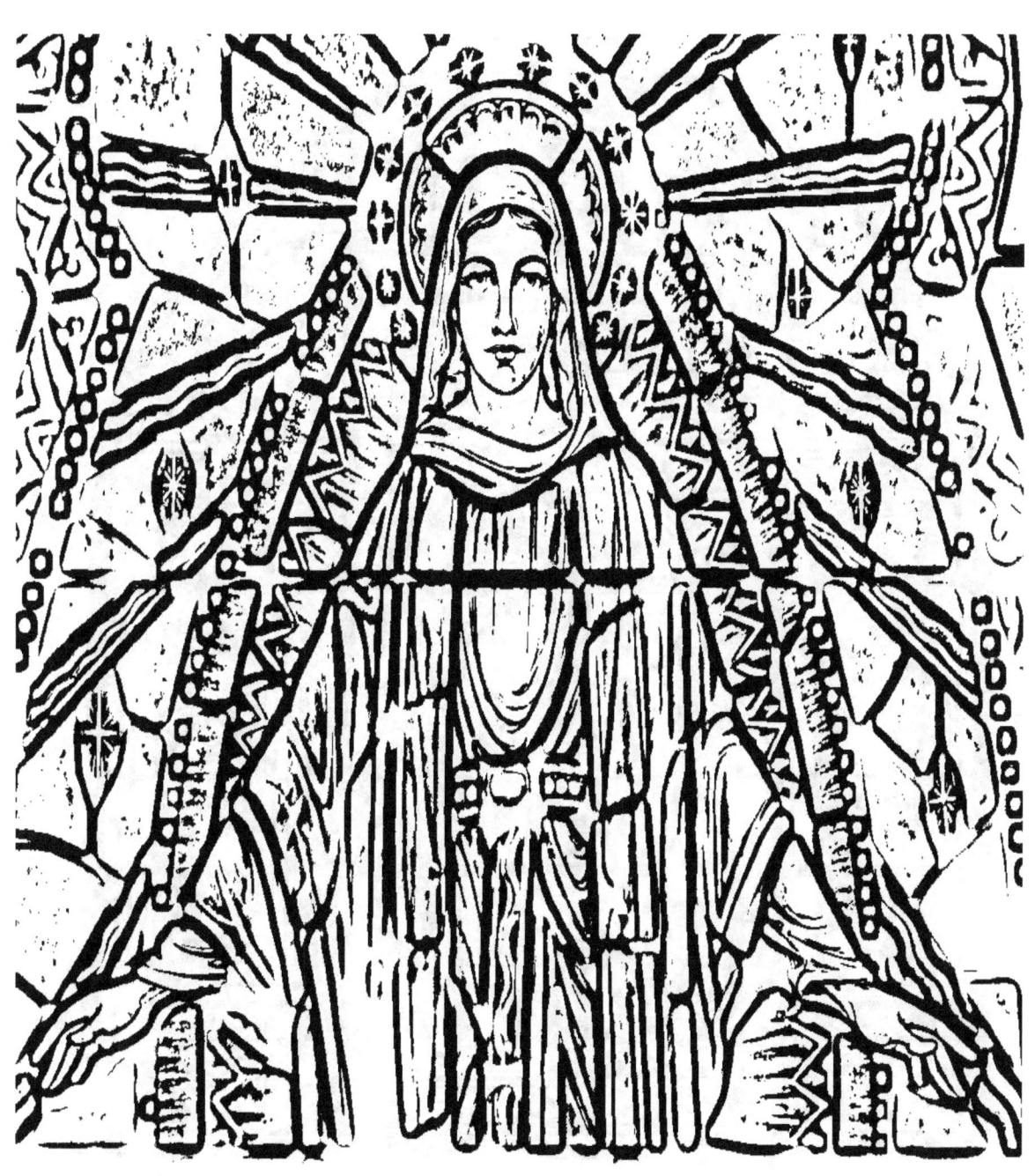

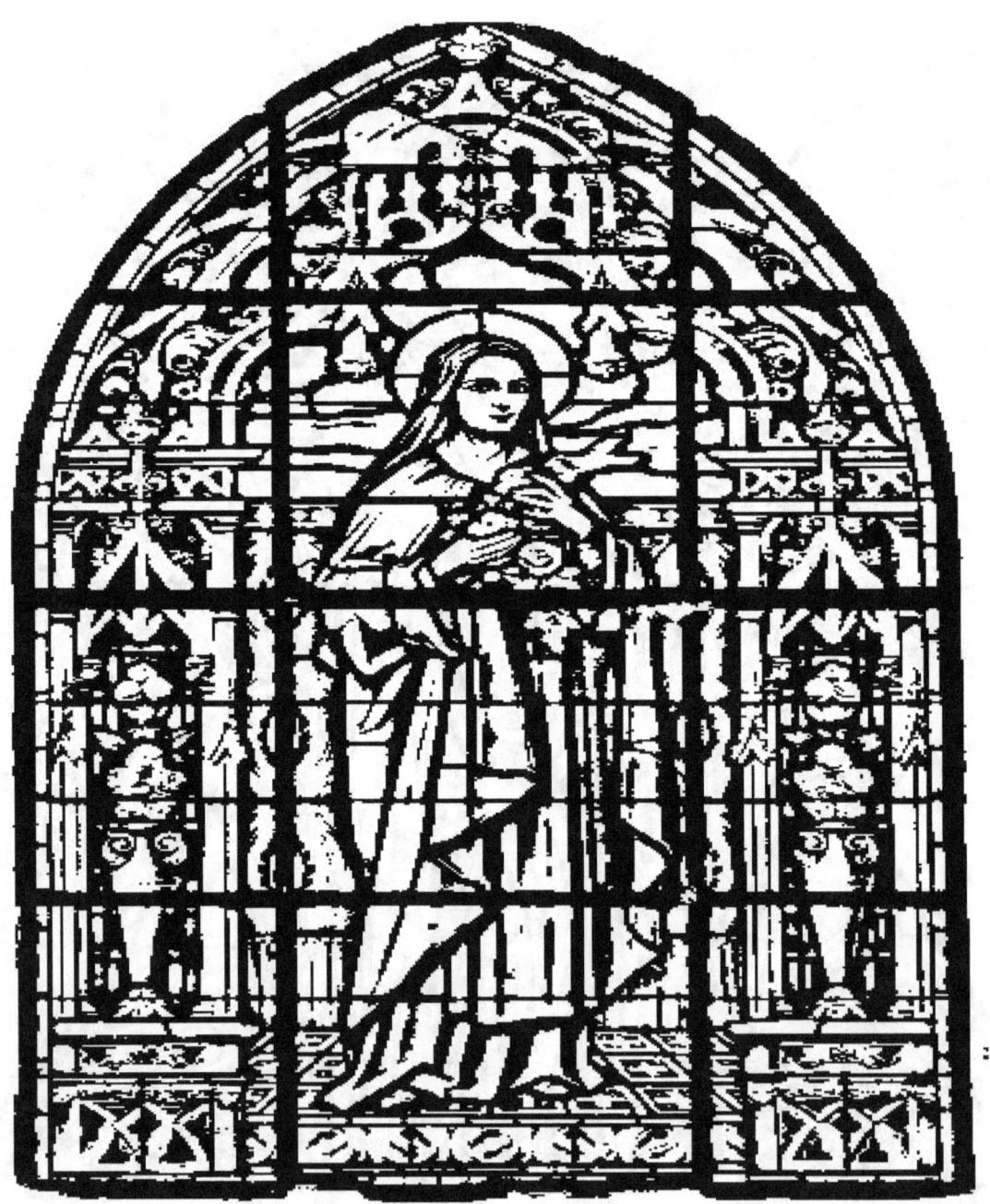

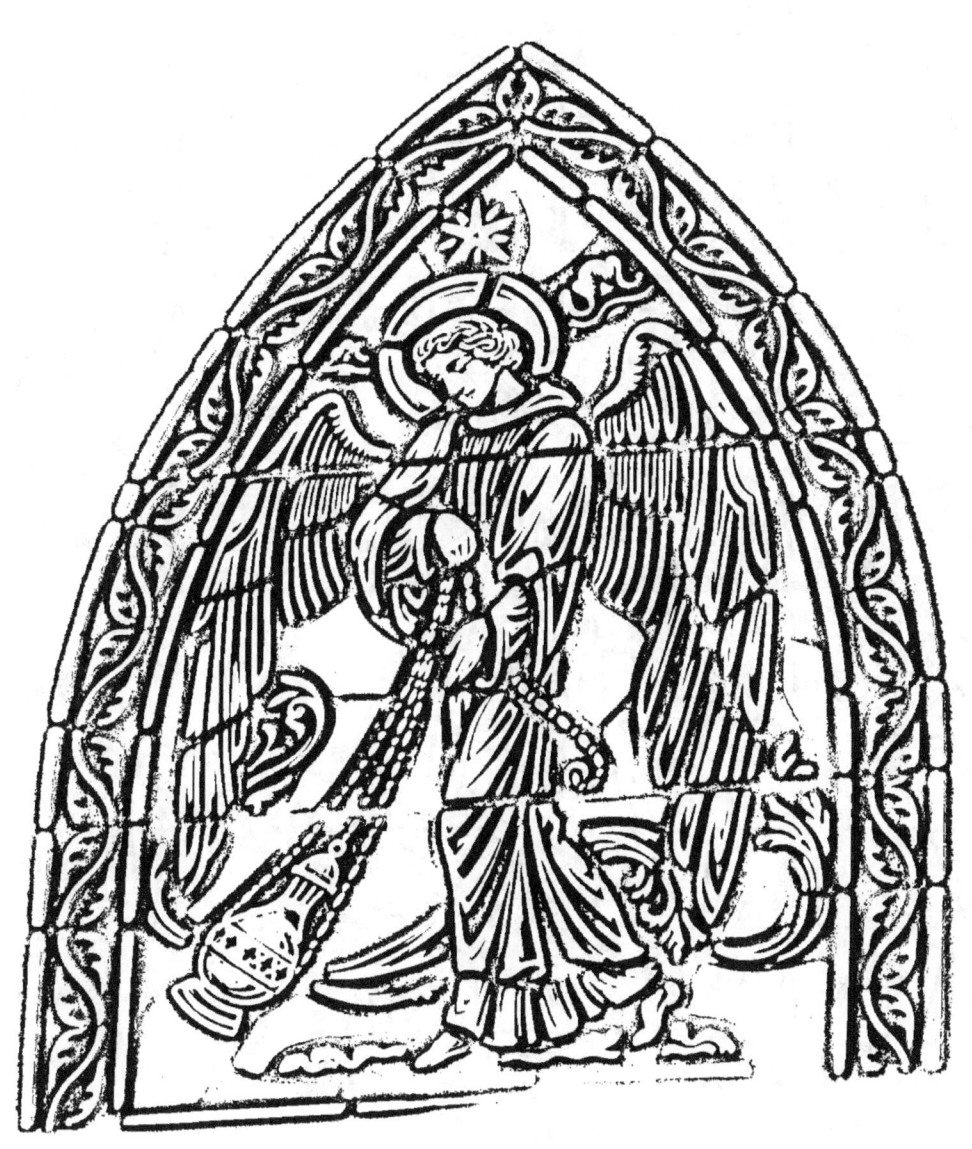

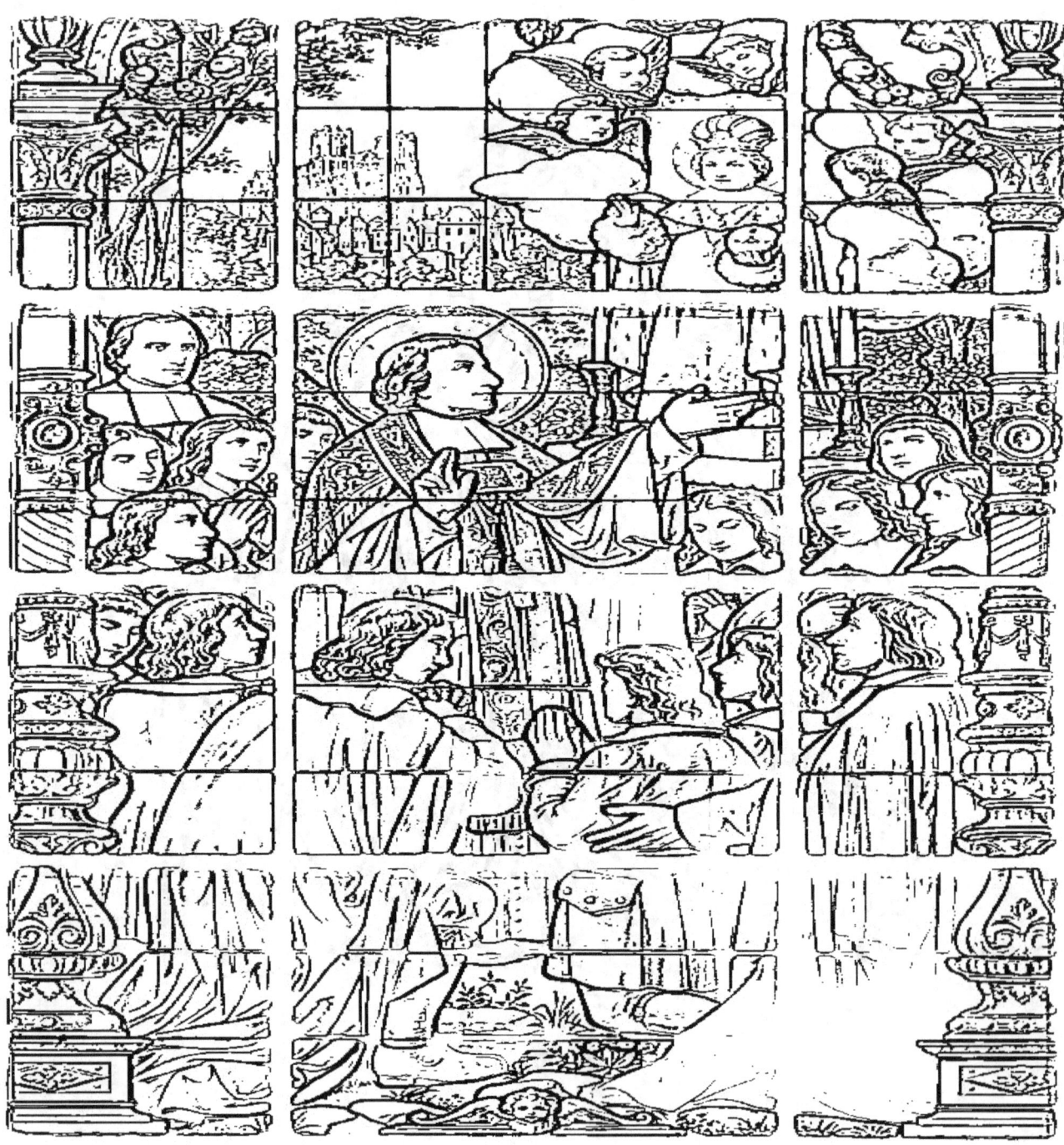

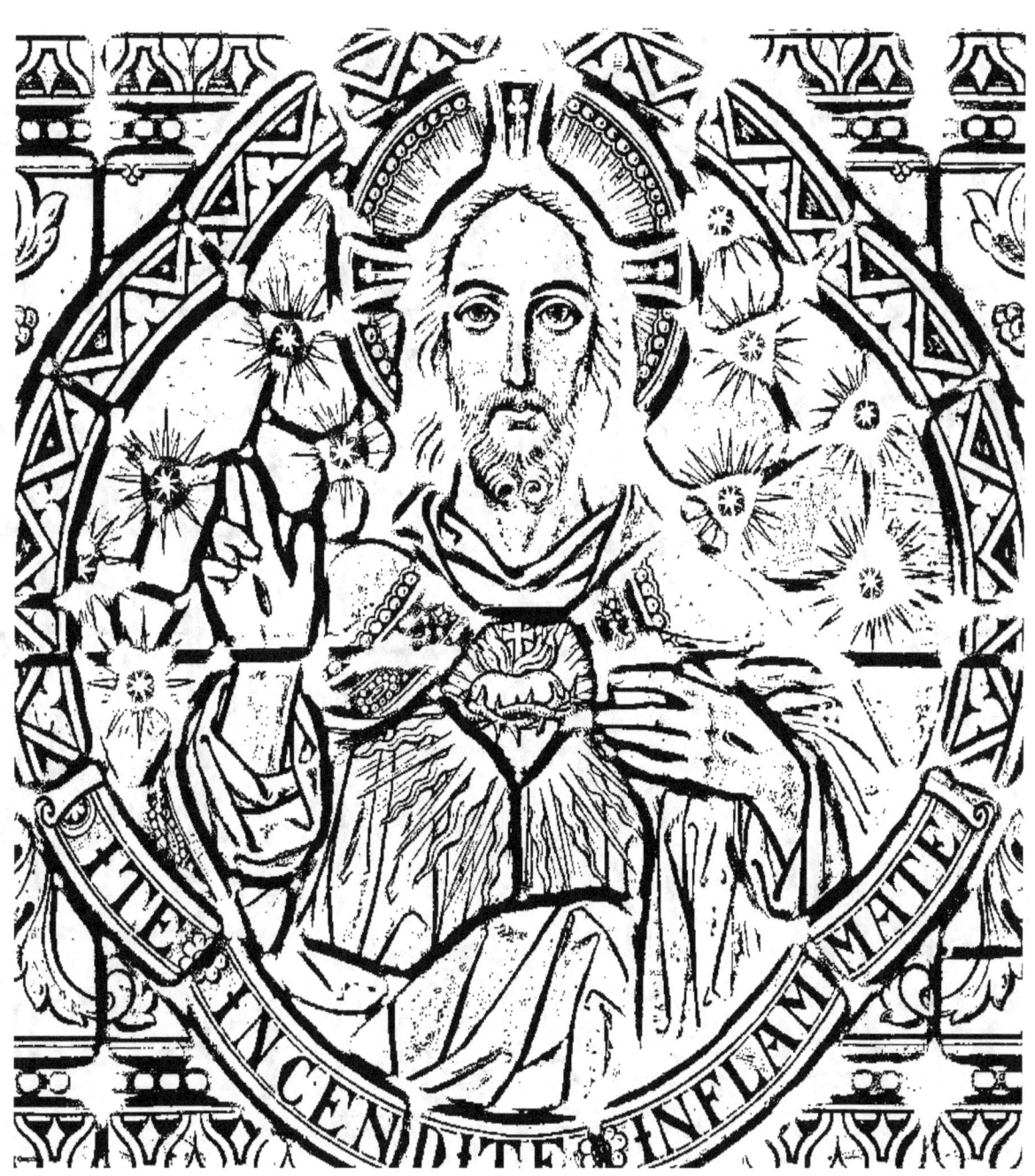

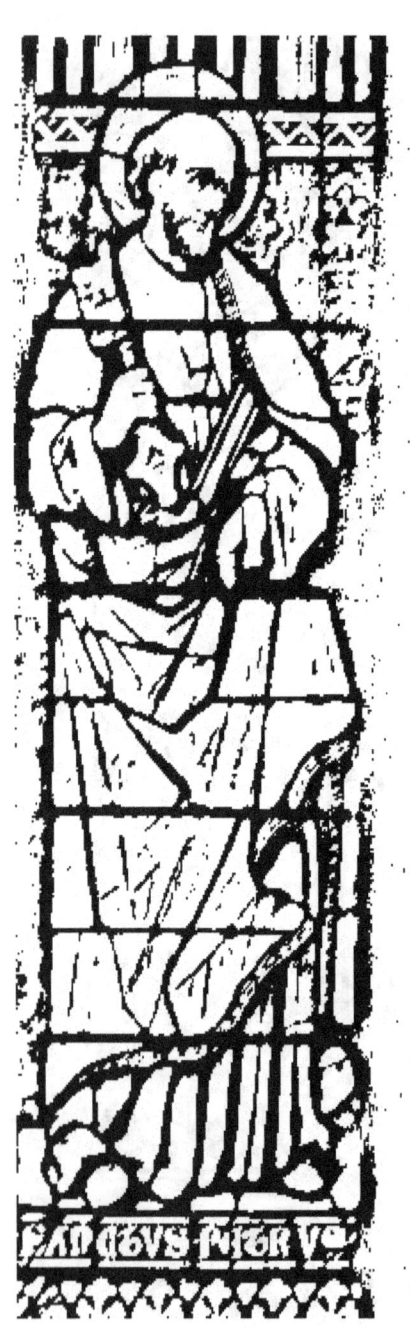

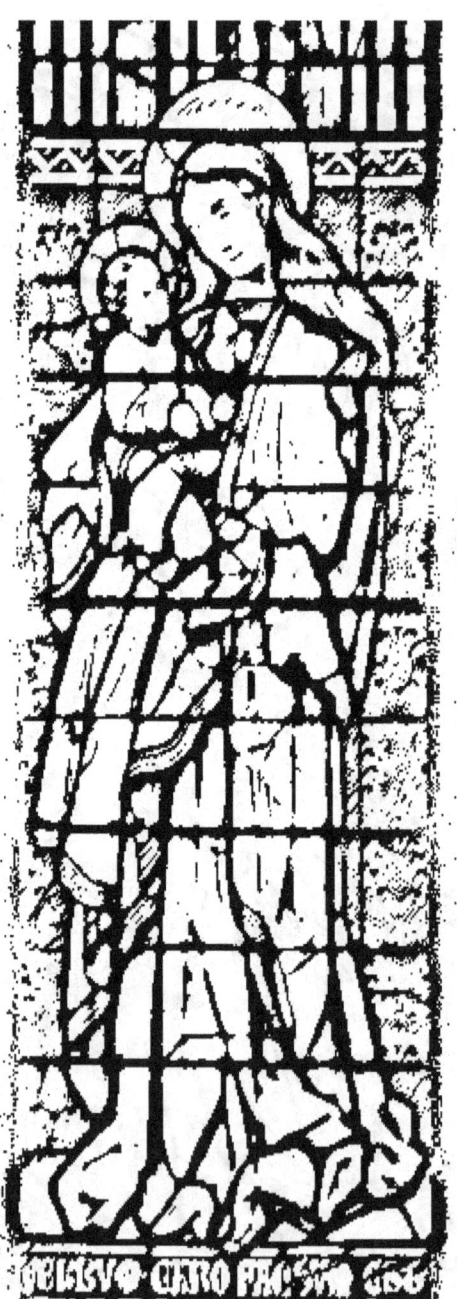

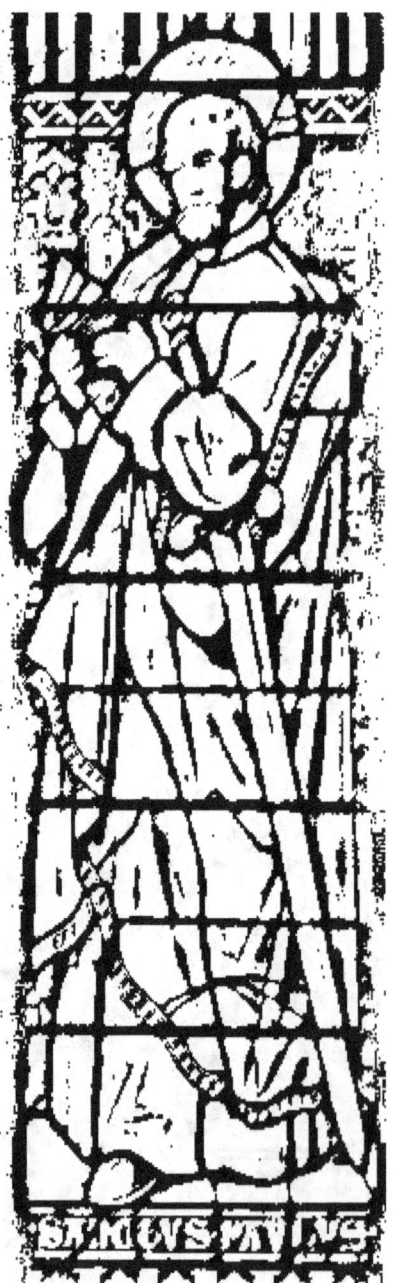

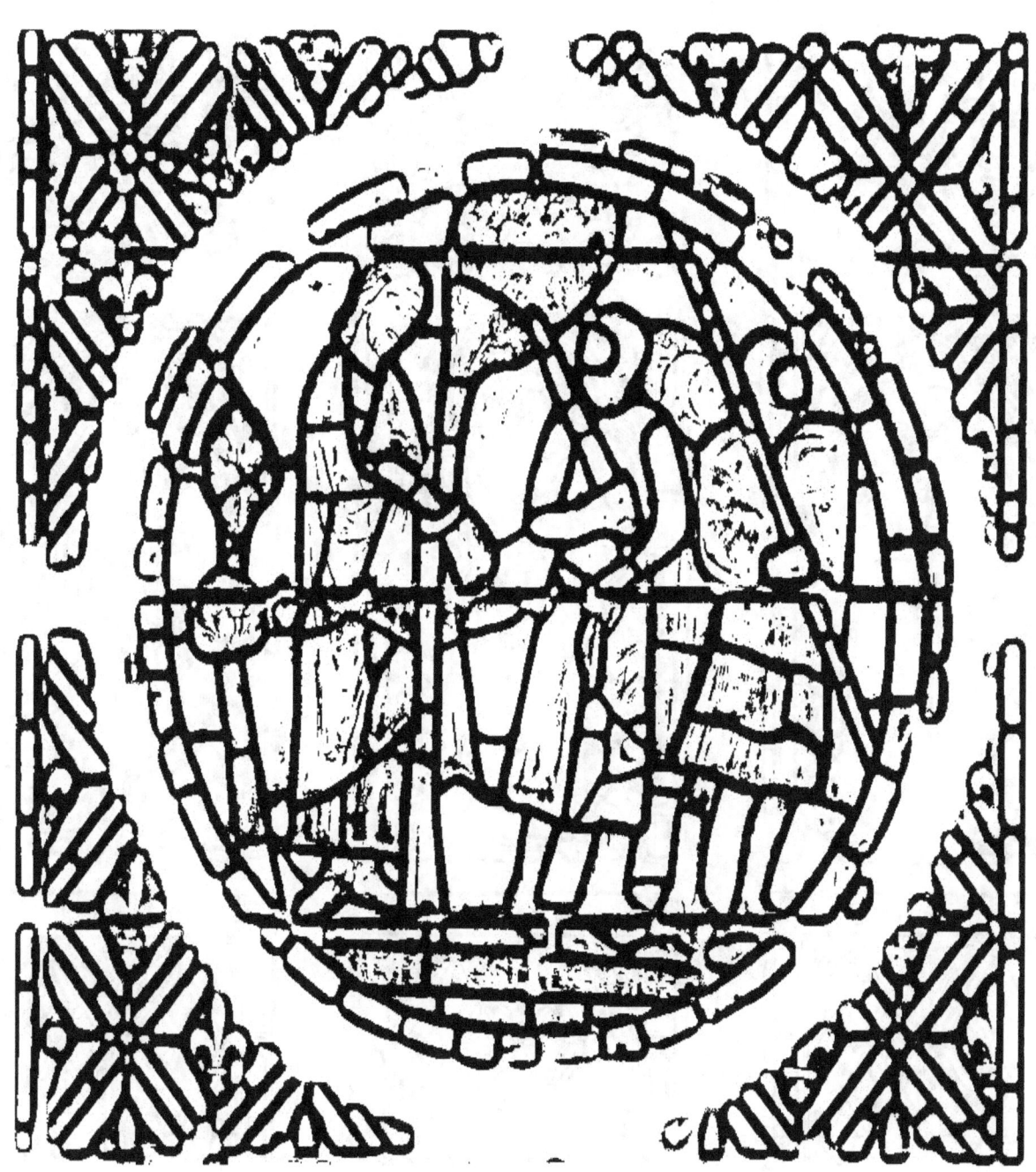

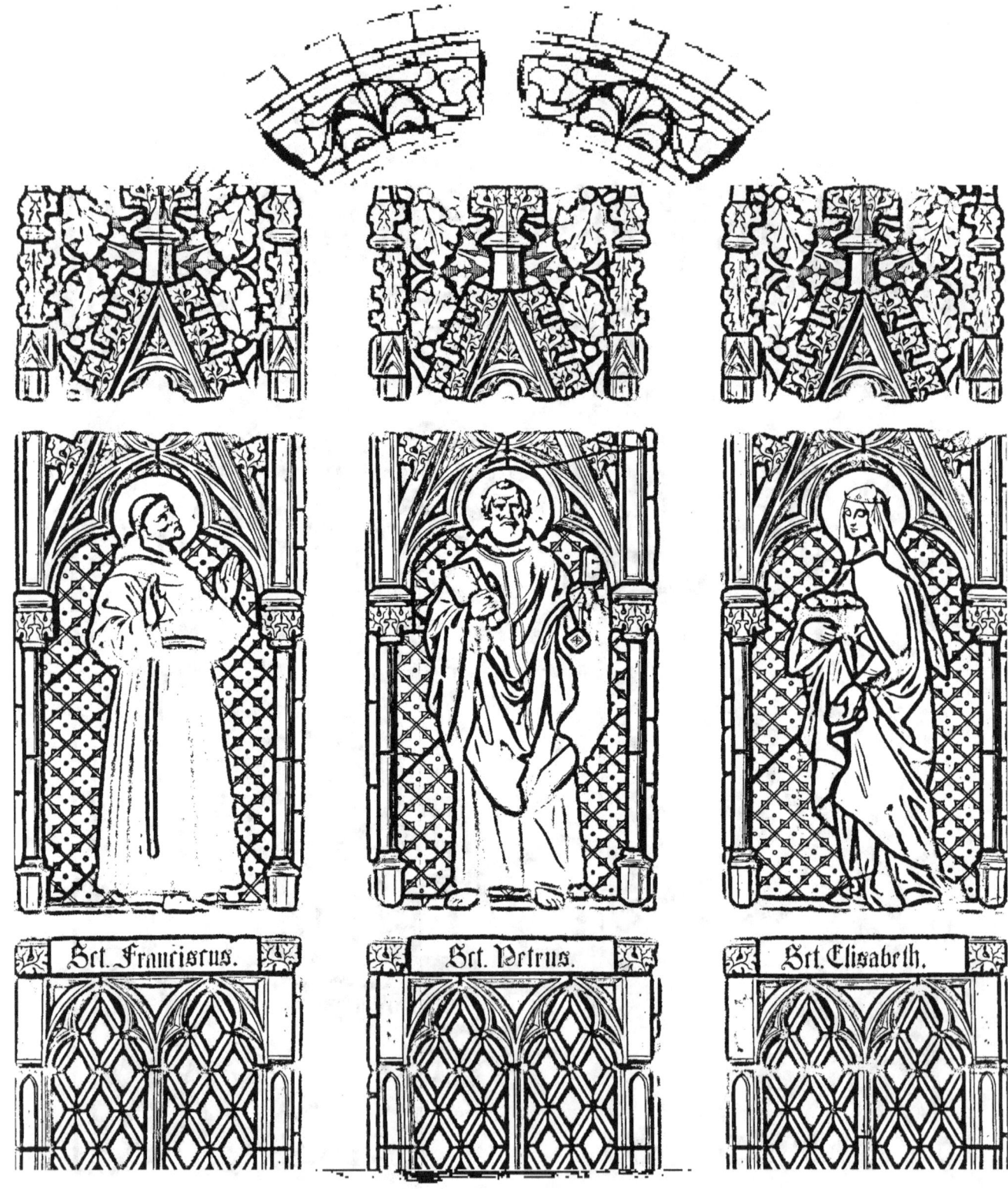

Sct. Franciscus.     Sct. Petrus.     Sct. Elisabeth.

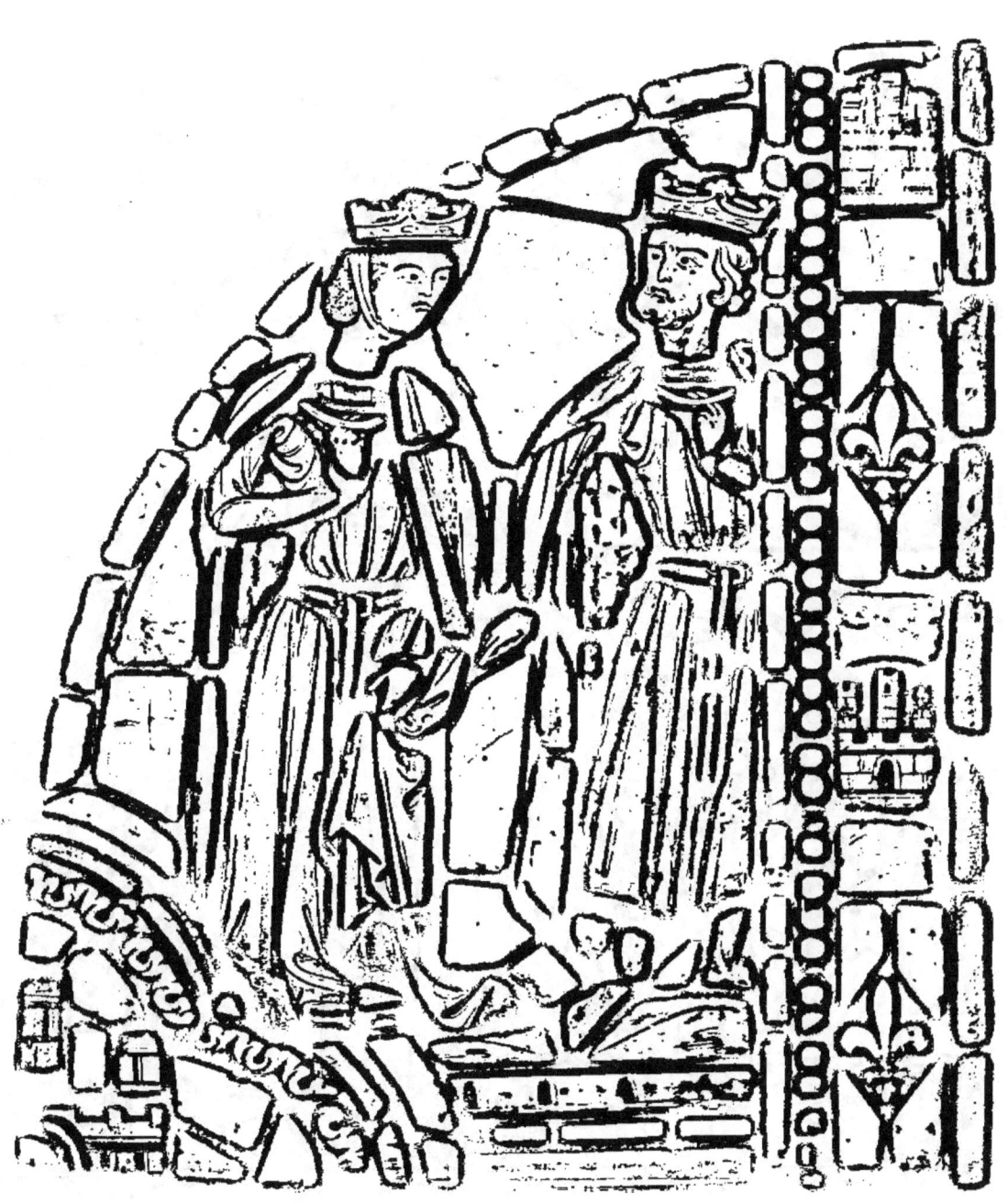

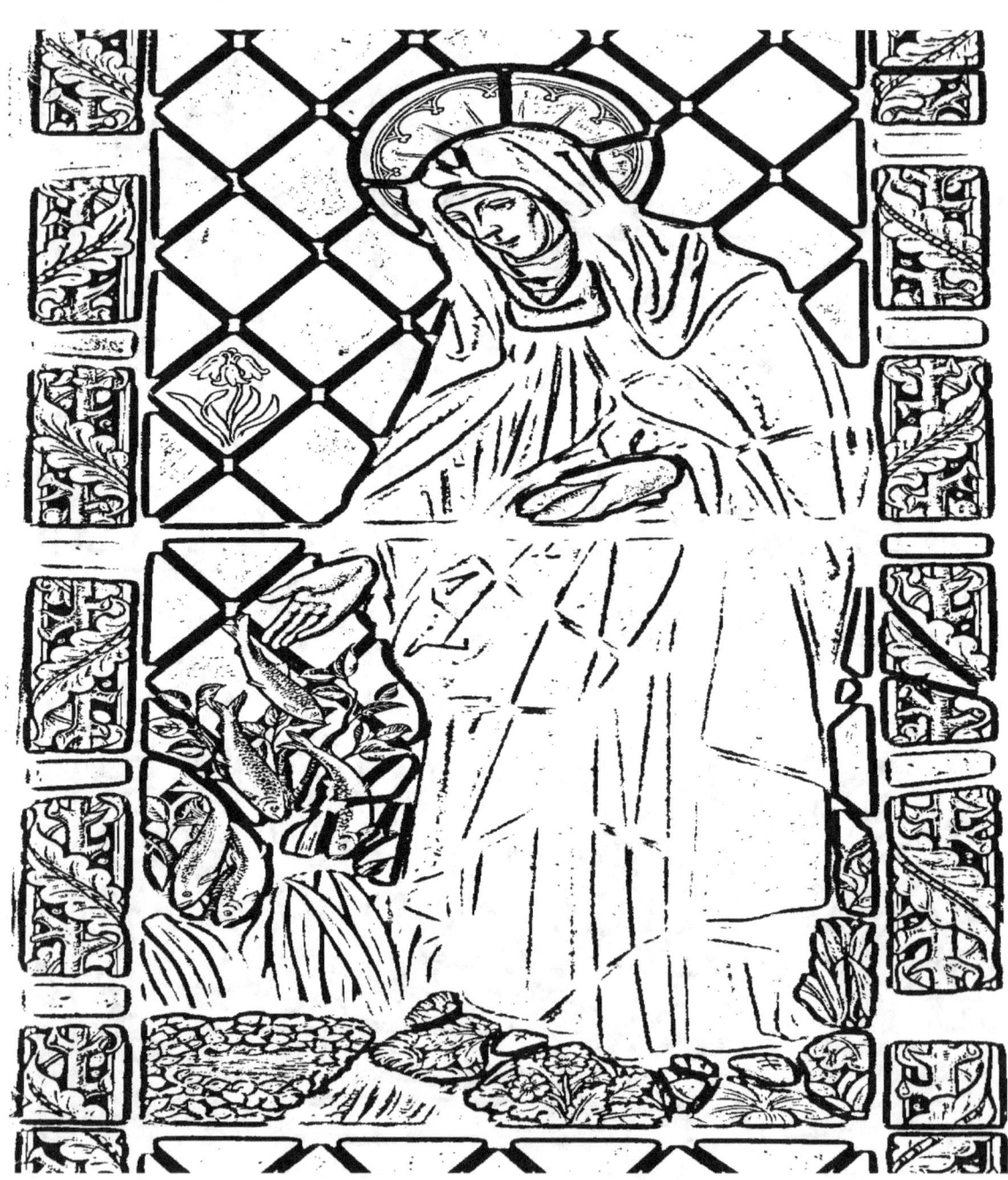

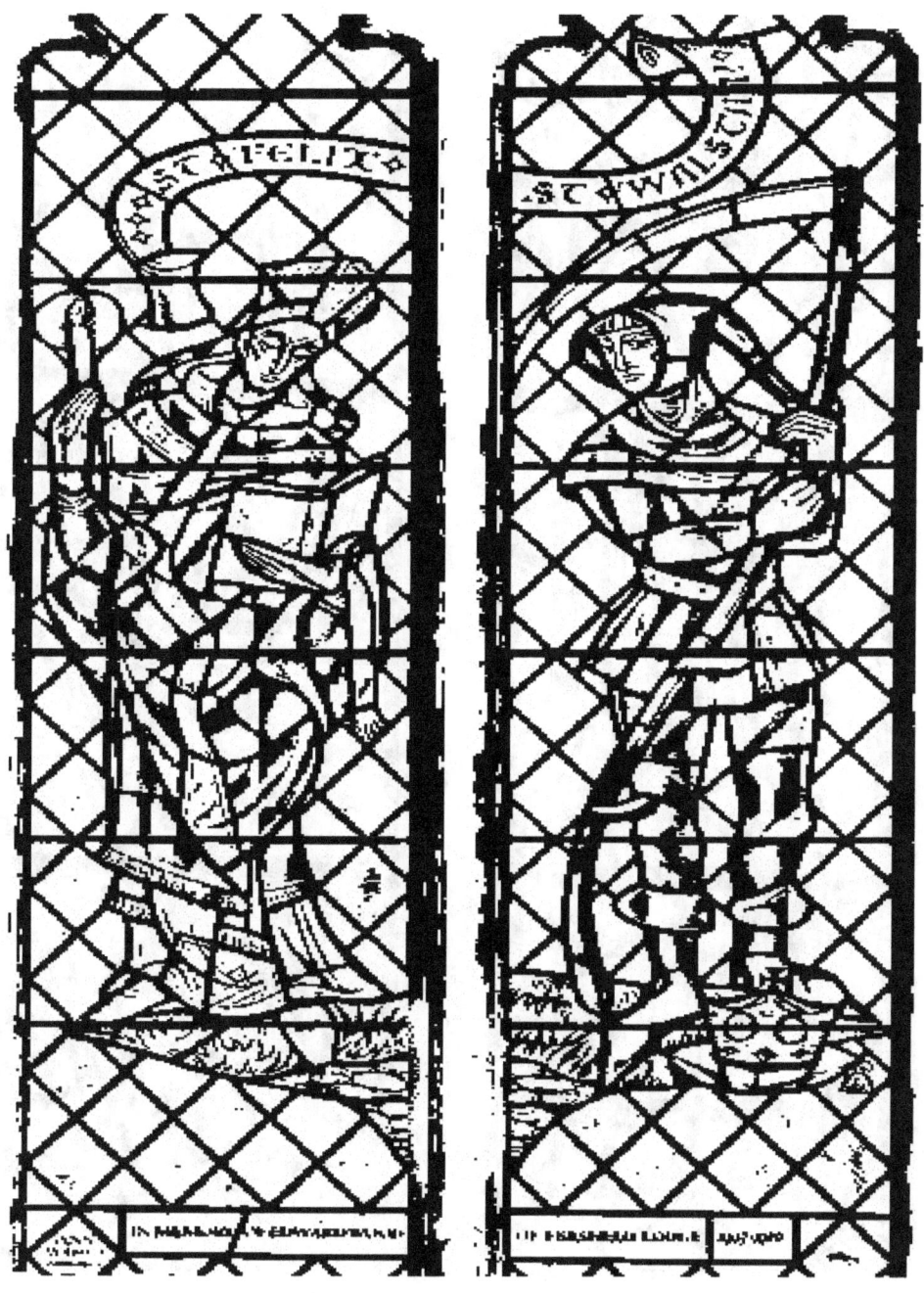

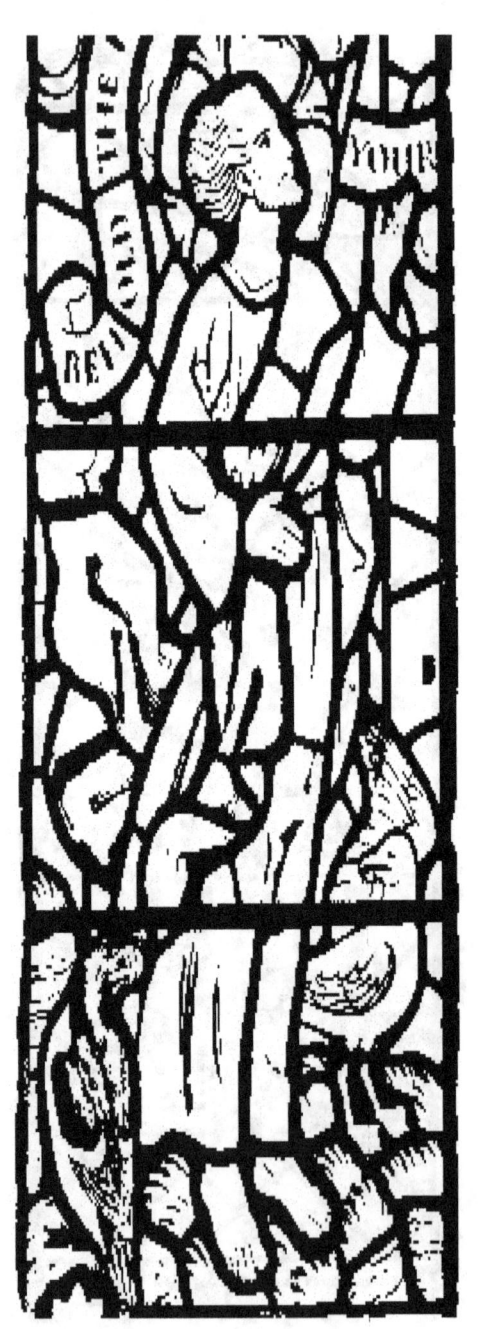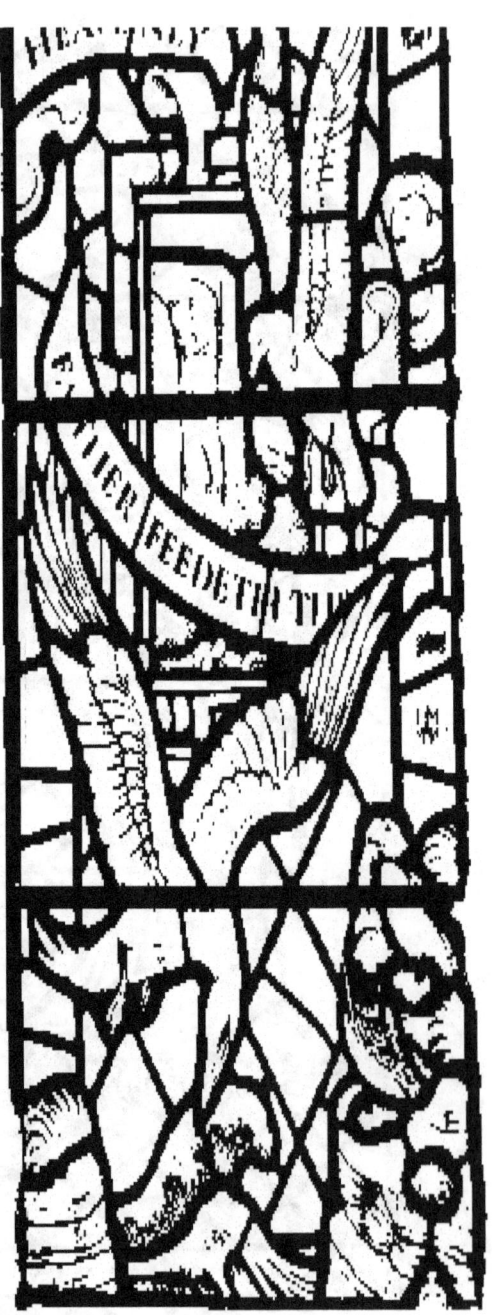

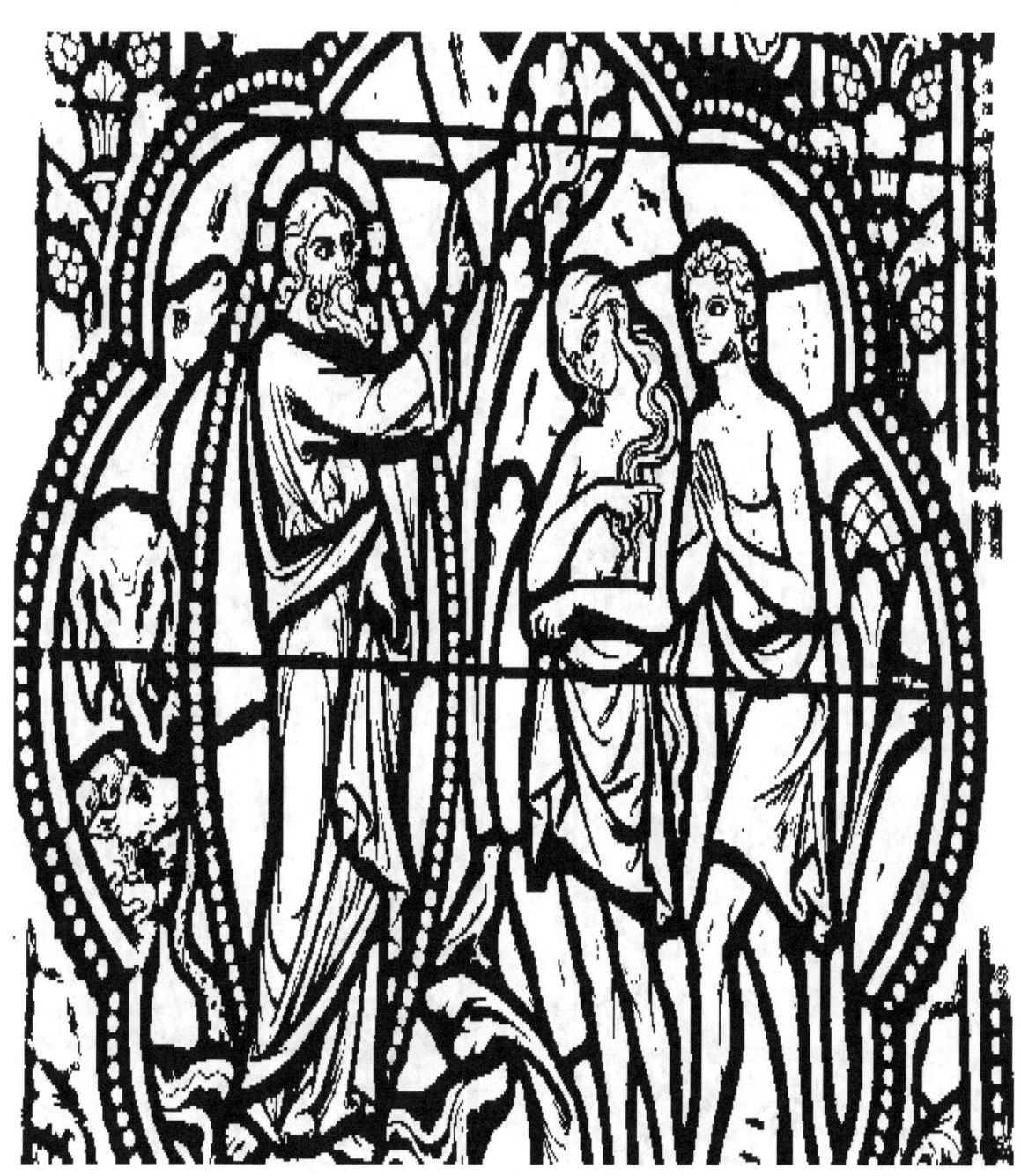

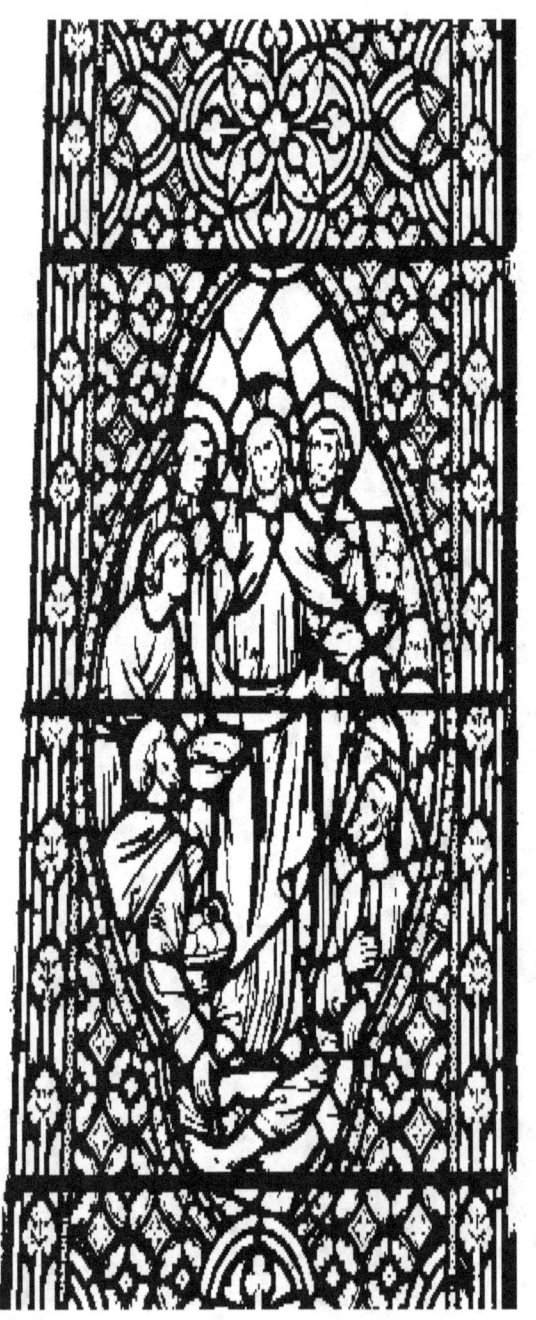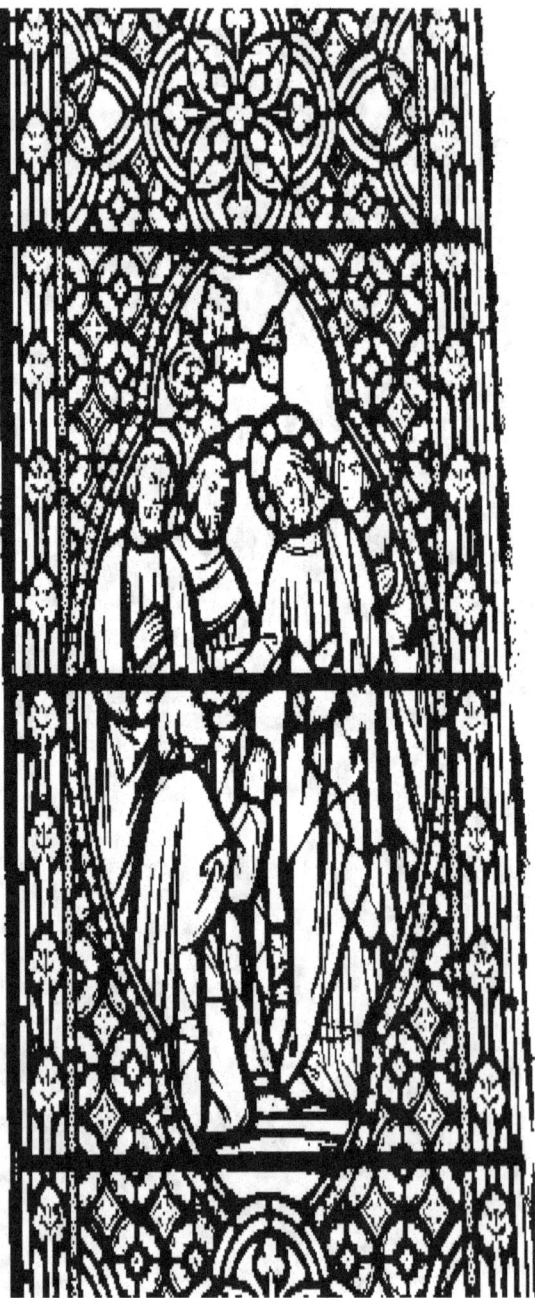

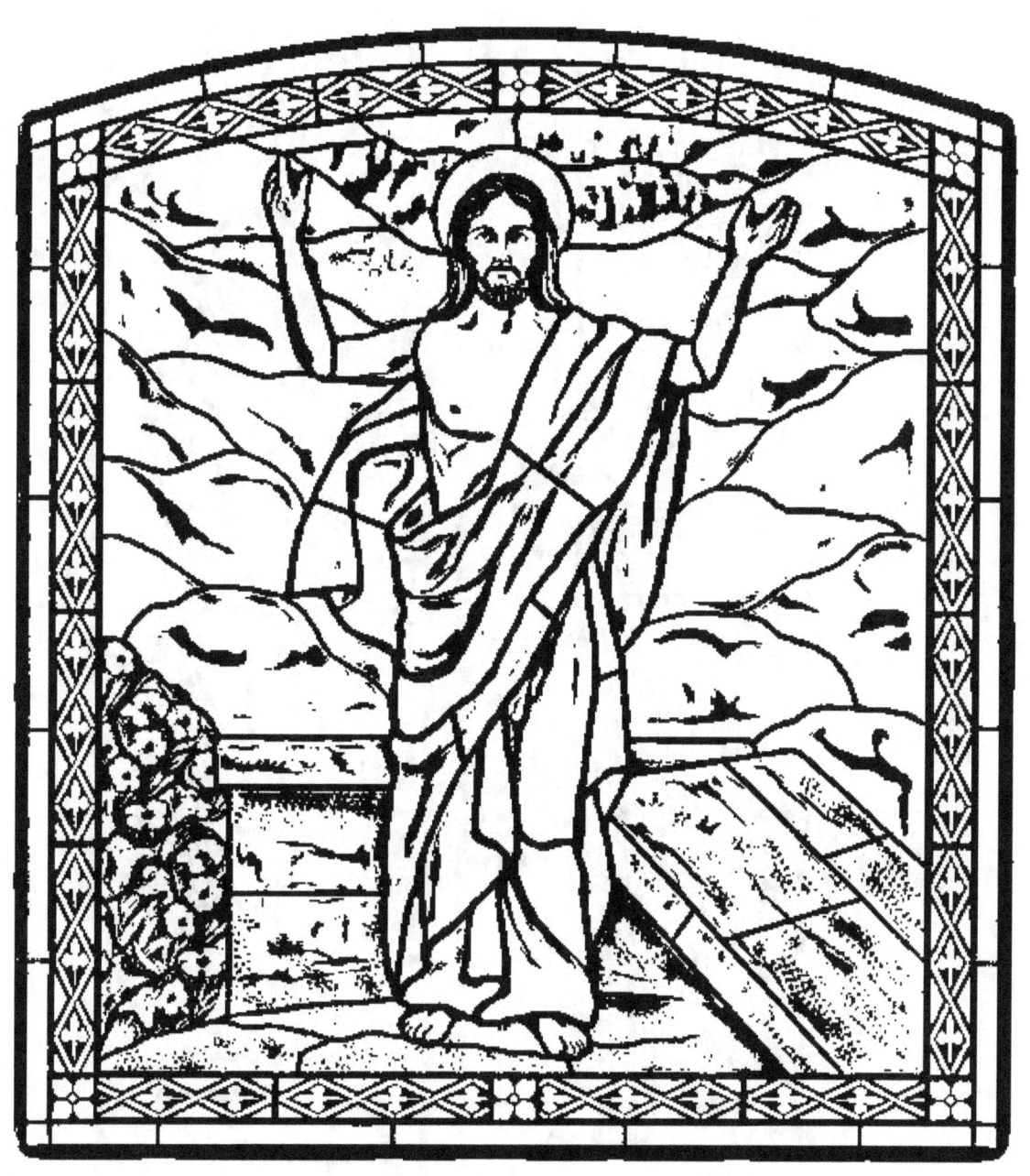

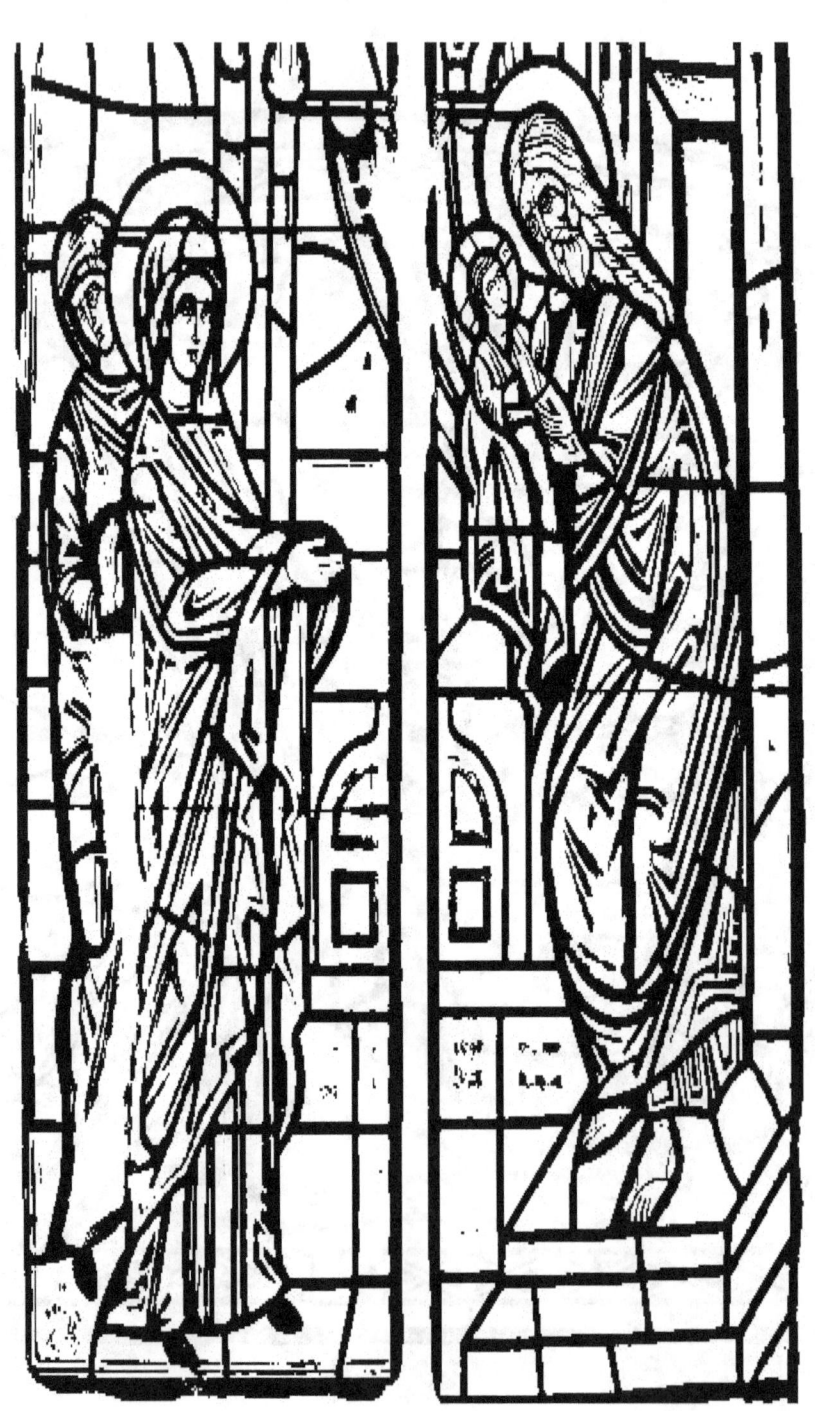

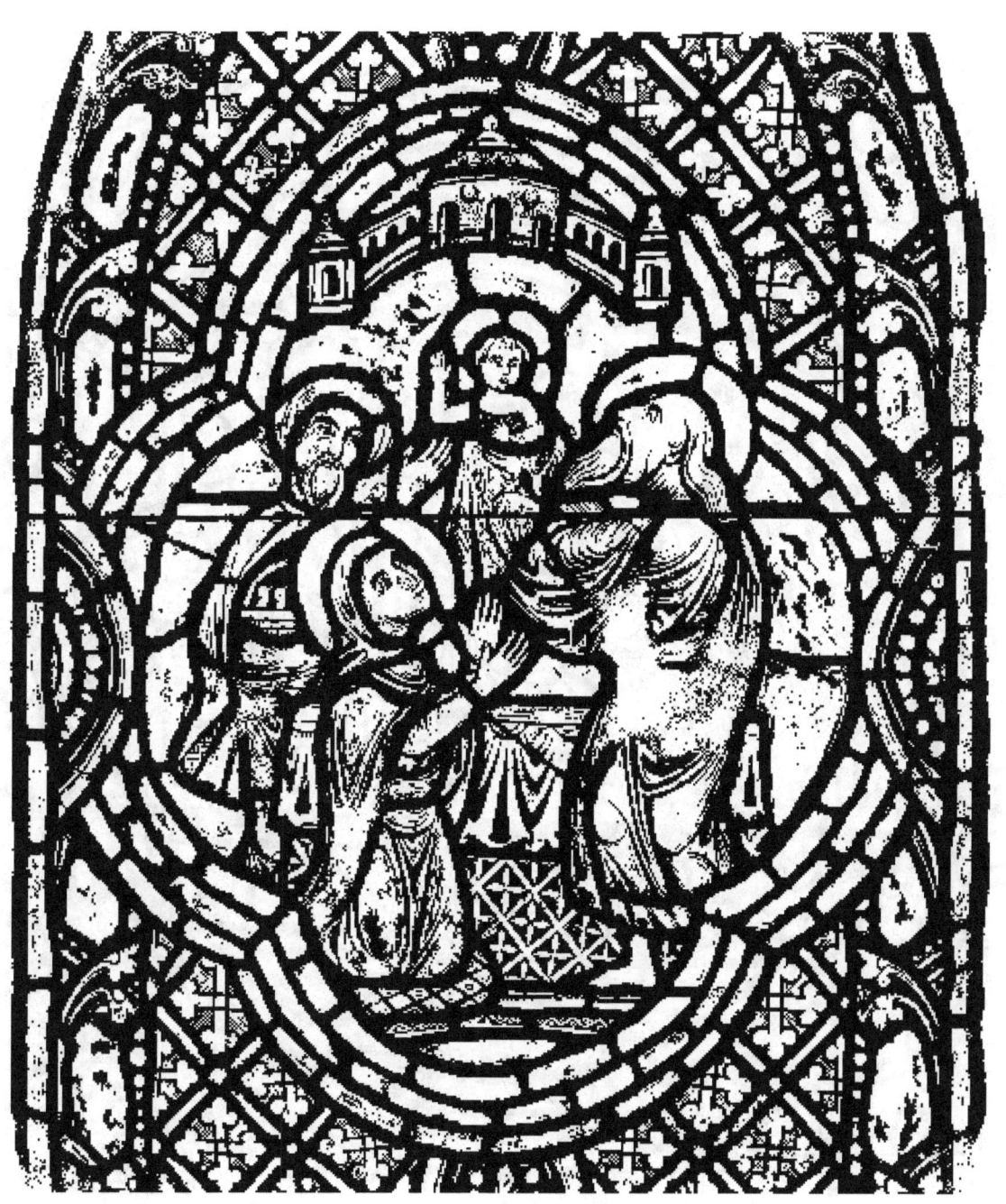

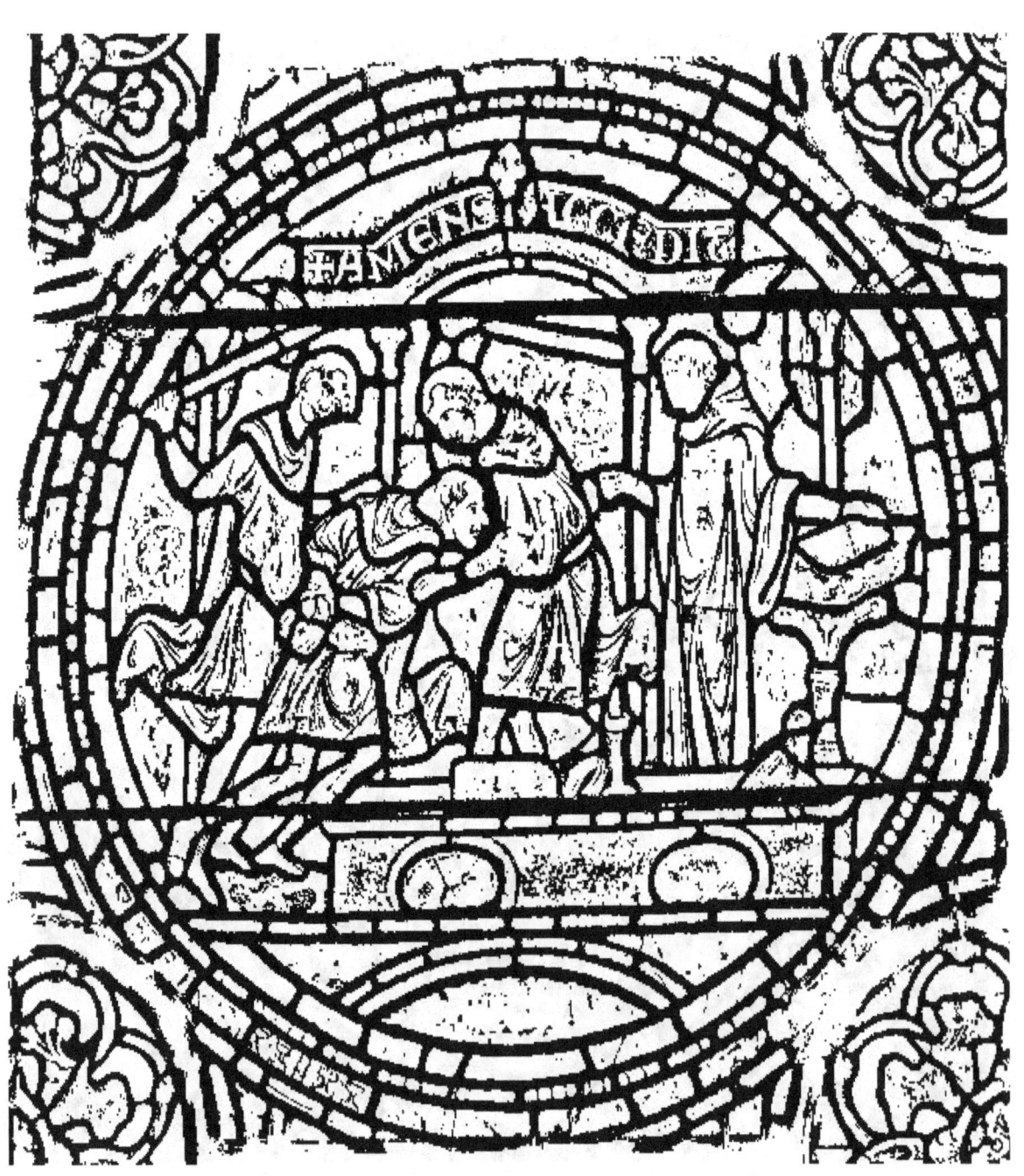

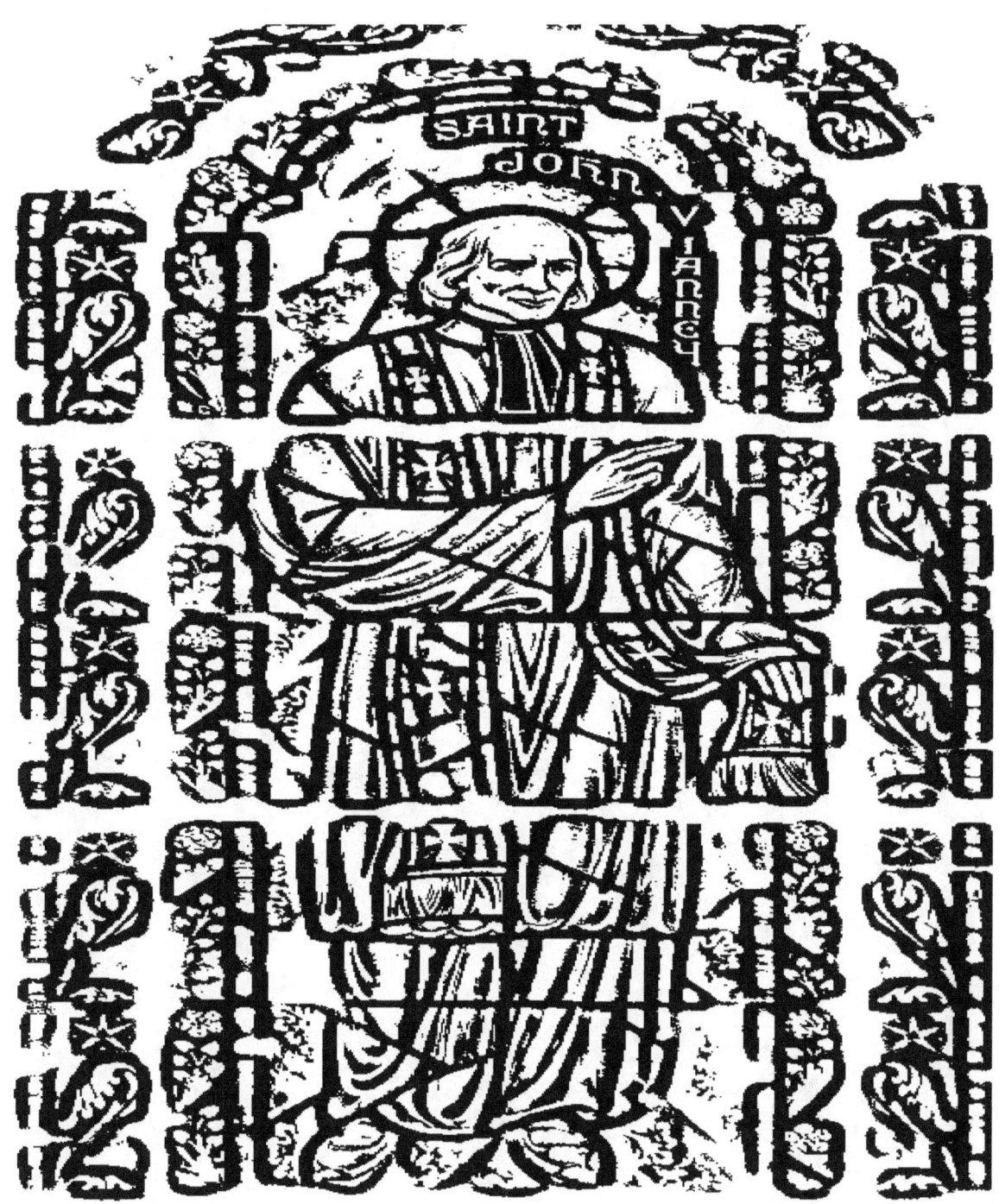

www.ingramcontent.com/pod-product-compliance
Lightning Source LLC
Chambersburg PA
CBHW081621170526
45166CB00009B/3062